GIVE

GIVE YOUR GUEST
A
wow!

21 Ways To Create Impeccable Hotel Customer Service That Leaves A Lasting Impression

ADAM HAMADACHE

R∃THINK PRESS

First published in 2013 by Rethink Press
(www.rethinkpress.com)

Front cover design by Martin Buchan
(illuminati-design.co.uk)

Dedicated to Margaret, Louis and Olivia.

Without their unyielding support and belief,
I would not be where I am today.

Thank you.

What's Been Said About Give Your Guest A WOW!

"This book gives a real insight into elevating the guest experience to new levels. Adam Hamadache's clever tips and well thought through strategies will be of real benefit to those in the hotel industry!"

Janice Gault, CEO, Northern Ireland Hotel Federation

"I was hooked in the first page of the introduction. Adam has brought back the meaning of hospitality, something the industry has lost some of its reputation for over the years. Simple, thoughtful ideas that will put the WOW back in the guest experience at any hotel."

Ciara Feely, Hotel Conference Expert

"Adam has produced a practical and thought-provoking set of ideas in this book. Great for newcomers and a timely reminder for seasoned operators."

John Gallery, the Great Potential Marketing Consultancy

"Adam Hamadache's book is a must read for every hotelier. Packed with practical, simple ideas to create a powerful impression on customers, it made me wonder why no one had thought of them before! I can imagine that soon the hospitality industry will be divided into those who have read this book and those who have not… and I pity those in the latter camp!"

Elizabeth Marsh, Founder, Elizabeth Marsh Floral Design

"If you'd like to get more repeat business and referrals for your hotel (and let's face it, who wouldn't), read this book. Adam has included a host of practical ideas (with plenty of illustrative examples) to WOW your guests and, most importantly, get them talking about you and coming back for more. Many of these are so simple and easy to implement you'll be kicking yourself you haven't thought of them before. And the best bit, many of them will cost you next to nothing (if anything) to do."

Caroline Cooper, Co-Author, *The Hotel Success Handbook*

"In as little as four hours you could be on the way to changing your hotel for the better, and creating WOW Moments for your guests! A real page turner, great ideas and so easy to implement. This book is an essential tool for every hotelier!"

Amanda Kennedy, Kenzia Restaurant Marketing

"'Give Your Guest a WOW!' is loaded with real-life examples, practical advice and helpful tips that hotels in all segments can implement tomorrow to create remarkable, shareable and memorable guest experiences."

Daniel Edward Craig, Author and Founder of Reknown

Connect With Adam

Twitter:	@adamhamadache
Email:	Adam@wowguest.com
Blog:	www.wowguest.com/blog
Website:	www.adamhamadache.com
	www.wowguest.com

CONTENTS

Introduction

For many years I've been helping hotels to drive bookings. I've done this by being commissioned by mainstream national newspapers and magazines such as *The Times*, *The Daily Telegraph* and *The Daily Express*, creating promotions such as 'save up to 50% off', whereby the reader is exposed to hundreds of hotels at great prices. The principle of these promotions is very simple: the hotel invests a small fee (typically the cost of one or two bookings) in an attempt to drive new customers to their hotel. Paying no commission. Hotels involved range across the board, from the quaint, five-bedroom, family run country B&B to the boutique, centrally located five star hotel, and everything in between.

These promotions represent a good opportunity to acquire customers. The unfortunate thing is that most hotels don't want customers, they want a sale.

Let me explain. A sale is when you sell a product or service: the end. A customer is when you have someone who is interested enough to buy from you:

- They buy that particular product or service
- You ensure that product or service is delivered as effectively as possible
- You build and nurture the relationship with the customer
- They buy from you again, in the same or a different way, and
- They recommend and refer business to you

When you want a customer you're happy to invest large sums, dip into your margin or even spend more than the cost of the initial product or service, because you know that, if you do things right, the big win lies in the lifetime value of that customer, not the value of that first sale. On the other hand, when you want a sale, you eat into your margin, you get the sale and that's it. There's no major incentive to produce a customer experience that is truly remarkable, no need to develop a relationship – you've got what you wanted from them, now you want them out as quickly as possible so you can make a new sale.

This book is intended to be read by hoteliers who want a customer, not just a sale – just so we are clear.

See the pattern here?

Another thing that continues to baffle me is a distinct lack of measurement. Whether the hotel, or any business come to think of it, spends money on marketing to acquire new customers or new sales, if that initial investment is not measured, you might not have bothered. If I had a penny for every time I asked a hotel how the promotion performed for them, and they couldn't answer, I'd be a very rich man. The most fundamental principle of marketing, bar none, is measurement. Without measuring the return on any investment made to acquire new customers, how on earth are you to know if it worked? And if you should do it again? More ludicrously, there will be businesses all over the world right now, spending money on the standardised marketing for their industry, over and over again, and it's not bringing them a single thing. Being able to track, precisely, where your sales and leads are coming from is just about the bread and butter of any business. I had a meeting not long ago with the marketing team of a well-known hotel group and when I started talking about tracking numbers and tracking URLs, they looked at me blankly. Two very basic principles of marketing that allow you to measure each media used to market your product and determine which is the more effective were completely new concepts to a team that market a hotel group with a turnover of £20m+. Astounding.

Hotels represent a unique opportunity. Very few businesses can boast 24 hours, 48 hours, three days, a week, two weeks' worth of upsell opportunities like a hotel can. If I pay £150 to stay in a hotel on a business trip for two days, I could spend that again, or double, at the restaurant, the bar, the spa, the gift shop, room service, the minibar (depending, of course, on the facilities offered). Yet, I am astounded at just how poor the encouragement and incentive is to maximise my spend when I stay at a hotel. This is true across the globe. Now of course I don't want to be hounded every five minutes by a member of staff trying to flog me a massage that I neither want nor have time for, but it comes back to the customer acquisition again – the hotel have made a significant investment to get me there in the first place; why are they not putting offers in front of me that I can't refuse? This point is not about the hard sell, it's about allowing your guests to make an informed decision based on what's available to them, why they should visit the restaurant, bar etc, and typically an incentive to do so that is managed correctly. If this point resonates with you, we cover this in great detail; you'll find several WOW Moments you can implement *today* that help you increase the spend within the hotel.

Going back to the subject of wanting a customer, not a sale: when you spend money to acquire a customer, particularly in the hotel industry, you'll be looking for repeat sales in the medium and long terms. I just want to emphasise the importance here because, over the last decade, the hotel industry has been completely shaken up by the internet. Never have your customers been so savvy as to what constitutes a good deal. That means that prices and margins are being squeezed harder than ever, meaning that the cost of acquiring that customer has never been greater. Which, if you'll forgive me for labouring the point, means that the importance of maintaining a dialogue with that customer, building a relationship with them and making it really quite easy for them to return, absolutely must be the priority to ensure that the initial heavy investment to get them there in the first place was worthwhile. The reality is that most hotels are very poor at this. I receive hundreds of emails every month from my client hotels: hotels that I'm not currently working with, hotels that I've been a customer at, and very rarely do I see anything other than an opportunity to come back and stay for a fixed price point deal that represents good value. Now this will work, and I'm sure for many it does, but it's not doing much to build a relationship with *me*, nor is it giving me any value.

Think about this. What value could you offer to your previous guests other than X% off staying at your hotel? Well, to know the answer you really ought to know your customer. Let me give you an example:

I'll often squeeze in two or three golf trips a year with friends at various golf resorts in the UK or abroad. Now, I don't live and breathe golf, but if I stay once or twice at hotels like The Celtic Manor or The Belfry and I've played golf there, it wouldn't be unreasonable to assume that I might be interested to receive an e-mail offering me something like: *Seven secrets of a PGA professional* or *How to take five strokes off your game*. No sales pitch, no offer, just an e-mail with some helpful pointers. The next time I was offered a golf break, I might give it more thought...

Throughout the book, I share lots of WOW Moments that have an emphasis on easy, inexpensive implementation with fast, measurable results that actually serve to build a relationship with your customers.

The last point that I really want to hammer home before we get started on what I hope will be an eye-opening read is something I touched on at the start of the chapter – the customer. When you adopt the customer mindset, and not the sale mindset, you acknowledge that your service as a hotel is always, always, always about the customer. This book is written with the underlying principle that if you get the customer experience right, and I mean really right, then the other things like more spend in the hotel, more repeat bookings, more positive reviews on Trip Advisor (with a little help from the systems I share) will come too. I still find it hilarious and disheartening at the same time when I see emails sent from hotels, often beautiful properties worth tens of millions, sending emails out that contain the word 'newsletter' in the subject line. This a sure-fire way to show that the emails aren't being tracked for open and click through rates because, if they were, they'd realise how few people were reading them. The key thing here is that an email with news about the business is of no interest to your customers 99% of the time; a few copy tweaks makes it about them, your customer, not about you. It should never be about how great the hotel is, always about how great an experience the customer will have. Every process, every touch point and every element of your hotel experience should be geared towards ensuring that your guest has the *most* remarkable stay.

This book, at its core, is about providing an experience that surprises and *WOWs* customers way beyond their expectations. This will lead you to achieve more sales, more referrals, better reviews and more profit. Any hotel can achieve these things and I'll show you just how easy it can be. Here's to your success.

CHAPTER ONE

WOW Your Guests

Let me start by explaining what a WOW isn't. You might have read that and thought ok, well I do that already as my service is great. It may well be and, frankly, good service is the bare bones of what a WOW is. A WOW, that is, to WOW your guests, is:

An unexpected, personalised gesture that demonstrates appreciation of custom, leaving a lasting impression on the guest and helping to create a remarkable experience for that guest.

I could have chosen a more technical term to describe this sweep-you-off-your-feet, powerful euphoria, but somehow I think WOW does the trick.

WOWs make your guests *feel*. Most will simply arrive at a hotel and not really have thought much about why they chose your hotel; it looked nice, it was the cheapest, it was the best location. These aren't feelings, they're simply logical choices – WOW your guests and they begin to feel something towards your hotel. Executed well, they'll begin to feel appreciated, knowing they are going to be looked after; they will likely feel a sense of pride that they picked your hotel; they may even feel proud of themselves for having made the right decision. Likelihood is that if you WOW them, particularly early on, they'll begin to feel some kind of affinity for your hotel. Once you've started them on that track it can become very powerful indeed: they'll not only have an amazing experience, they'll be more likely to spend more, tell their friends and come again.

Importantly, a WOW is not an opportunity to sell. Whilst this book is quite overtly about getting your guests to spend more, it is expressly about doing everything within your power to ensure that your guests have the most remarkable experience. It doesn't matter whether you run a three bedroom B&B or you're the General Manager of a 900 room resort; whether you charge £20 per night or £2,000 per night. The principle is to have your guests at worst pleasantly surprised, at best WOWed beyond every measure imaginable, but essentially feel compelled to share their remarkable experience with everyone who will listen.

So how do the two work together if a WOW is not an opportunity to sell? You might be reading this thinking, 'How do I make money if I'm not trying to encourage them to spend more with me?' We'll come to that, but, for now, simply acknowledge that as soon as you try to sell your guest something, or even ask them to do something they wouldn't ordinarily do, you won't WOW them. Think of a WOW in its simplest sense: just an opportunity to show your guests you care about their experience. Nothing more.

A wonderful example of this I experienced in my youth whilst flying Virgin Atlantic to Florida and, whilst I didn't really appreciate it then, a colleague has since told me this story and it reminds me what a remarkable WOW it is. Sometime between meals on Virgin's long-haul flights, their cabin crew come round and give everyone a choc ice. That choc ice isn't accompanied with the in-flight catalogue of all the duty free you can purchase, it's just a choc ice. Nobody's flight would have suffered if it hadn't been there and nobody would have complained if they hadn't been given it, but for many it's a conversation piece; an unexpected, unconditional little treat. That is a WOW. Test it yourself. Ask friends, family and colleagues whether they have flown Virgin and ask them if anything stood out about the service.

So, hopefully this concept of a WOW is a little clearer in your mind. You might be reading this thinking, 'Yes, but it all sounds like a lot of effort, especially when, like the choc ice example, they won't miss it if it's not there.' Well, that WOW, as insignificant as it might seem, could well be the difference between what they say about their stay to others. I like to use the dinner party example, which applies not just to hotels, it applies to any business, any experience when you're a customer. Will this experience become a story at a dinner party? Or, at the very least, down the pub?

Broadly speaking, there are four instances when an experience does and doesn't become dinner party worthy. The Nice, The Disappointing, The Very Bad and The WOW.

The Nice

This is when a stay is pleasing: staff were friendly enough, rooms were clean, food was ok – it was all just a little average. Nothing's stand-out and certainly not remarkable – it's just a bit nice! This isn't going to make it to the dinner party conversation.

The Disappointing

Your guests are a little annoyed, a little disappointed, but it wasn't life shattering and frankly it wasn't so bad that they felt the need to say anything; they just won't come back, but equally they don't feel the need to actively put their friends off. This isn't going to make it to the dinner party conversation either.

The Very Bad

This time your guests are more than a little annoyed. They are extremely frustrated and borderline angry that they even bothered to spend any money with you. It might have been rude staff, poor cleanliness, terrible food – it could be all sorts, but these guests are leaving much more upset than when they walked in. This will almost certainly make the dinner party: these guests will want to hail from the roof tops about not visiting your hotel again, and they'll most likely go on a rant about how dreadful it was. Not a good place to be in.

The WOW

Your guests were more than overwhelmed: the experience was refreshing; there were a couple of things that the staff did that really made them *feel* (there's that word again) appreciated and cared for. It seemed like the staff went out of their way to make the stay amazing. Undoubtedly this is making it to the dinner party – but most importantly it will be one or two things that *really* stood out for them. A WOW stay will have its own choc ice. This is the one element that they will want to regale friends about and will, as a result, change a nice stay to a WOW stay.

Now let's say that you successfully administered a WOW stay. Well done you. A couple of days or even weeks later they are going to share the moment they were WOWed with friends at a dinner party, down the pub, over coffee etc. They want to share their experience because it meant something to them. They were so overwhelmed by those one or two WOW Moments, they'd never seen anything like that before, that when their friend or colleague or family member asks them, 'So what's new?' It will likely be the most notable thing that has happened in that recent time. This might seem a little far-fetched at first. That's fine. I expect a little scepticism. But just think back to the conversations you've had about somebody's experience of service of some kind: it might have been at the post office – the queues were horrendous (Very Bad). It might have been at the library – the nice librarian went out of her way to find me the book I was after (WOW). I challenge you not to comment, or hear a comment about a service in the next seven days. It happens. And when your customers are talking about you, you'll want to it be as a result of a WOW not a Very Bad.

Significantly, a 2012 Accenture report showed that the UK has the highest percentage of people telling their friends about poor experiences. They report that as many as 78% of people have told others about poor experiences and 20% posted online. Incentive enough to make sure you're not in the Disappointing or the Very Bad.

Let's take this a little further to really understand the potential behind these seemingly ordinary conversations. Let's assume you've successfully WOWed a customer. They tell that story of that WOW five times to five of their friends. That's 25 potential customers hearing favourable things about your hotel from a source they trust and whose opinion they value. That word of mouth marketing cost you very little (and we'll talk about cost later). All from just one satisfied customer.

What if that was 100 customers a month that you managed to WOW – 2,500 potential customers are hearing great things about your hotel from someone they trust every month. That's 30,000 a year.

You might be thinking, yes, this is all very nice but how many will actually go on to book. The reality is very few. Typically we find it is about 1%. 1% of 30,000 is 300. Let's assume that the average booking is £150.

£150 x 300 = £45,000 in additional revenue.

By the way, these are very modest figures; chances are that the entire spend per booking is more than £150 depending on your size, price and upsell opportunities. All from simply doing your utmost to engage with your guests and WOW them with innovative WOW Moments.

Delivered and administered in the right way, a WOW will build that much needed relationship with your guests. This will only be achieved if your WOW attempts aren't sales pitches. As discussed before, a WOW attempt ceases to be a WOW if you're trying to get your guests to buy something, or do something they really don't want to do – a feedback request after a stay is a typical example. WOWs demonstrate that you are prepared to go out of your way, above and beyond what is required, to ensure the guests' stay is nothing short of inspiring.

This trust can lead to a higher spend, provided you give your guests the right opportunities to buy. It's the age old adage that you are more likely to buy from someone you like as opposed to someone you don't. In a business to business context, the emphasis on building relationships is so important and it's exactly the same with your guests. Build those relationships, create rapport with your WOWs and your guests will be more inclined to spend more with you.

You may have got to this point and are wondering, well, how do you create one of these WOWs. It's really not all that difficult, or expensive.

Within the next few chapters I'll start to share, but first I want to illustrate that human beings are really quite easy to WOW. Imagine walking into two different coffee shops, approaching the barista in each and asking for a coffee. The first barista doesn't acknowledge you and you find yourself standing at the counter for nearly a minute before they turn around and stop talking to their colleagues. When they finally do turn around, you barely get a grunt, just a half-hearted attempt to greet you. Whilst serving you they continue their conversation with their colleagues, completely ignoring your attempt to also request a cake with your coffee. You pay, get your coffee and your cake and leave. Sound familiar?

Now in the second coffee shop you enter, before you've barely got through the door and even before you've started making your way to the counter, you are greeted by a beaming, personable barista. They ask you how you are and what they can get for you. They initiate relevant, friendly conversation whilst taking your order and ask you if you'd like anything else with your coffee. When it arrives, you're told to enjoy and if it's not 100% perfect to let them know and they'll do it again for you.

It's all simple stuff. But let's be clear; we're looking at Disappointing and Nice experiences. Neither of these stories is making its way to the dinner party. If the first barista spilt the coffee all over you, it might make the conversation at the dinner party but that's not the direction we're interested in. Now consider this: whilst the second barista is serving you she offers you a small gourmet chocolate for free. She explains that these chocolates are completely Fair Trade, organic and they tested 50 chocolates and found that this was the winner; she hopes you enjoy your award-winning chocolate. That's a WOW.

That chocolate represents a personal, non-committal gift showing appreciation for your custom and a willingness to offer the very best to their customers – nothing more. It's not an opportunity to sell, it's not rewarding an additional purchase, simply an unexpected WOW Moment that has WOWed you.

Now, imagine that barista gave you a voucher with your purchase that offered you 25% off. That's a welcome gift, but let's be clear: it's not a WOW. Nobody is getting home, going to a dinner party and telling their friends about a '25% off your next coffee' voucher! But they might about being offered an award-winning chocolate!

CHAPTER TWO

UNDERSTANDING YOUR GUESTS' EXPECTATIONS

As I've discussed before, WOWs are unexpected. You don't WOW a guest by just employing staff who are polite, or just not rude. You need to do something that demonstrates just how important the guest's stay is to you that they would not necessarily expect. And it needs to be personal. Or something they've never experienced at any other hotel.

It might seem like a big task. But it just requires a little thought. Now, depending on the type of hotel you have/work in, the difficulty in successfully WOWing guests will vary hugely. It is much harder to WOW guests when expectations are high. When expectations are high some WOW gestures or moments that you tailor into the experience may be perceived as expected. For example, if a guest has paid in excess of £300 per night for a room, a complimentary shoe-shining service would probably not offer a moment that WOWs the guest. At that price, for what is largely a bed for the night, this kind of service would be expected.

On the other hand, if a guest pays less than £50 for a room and they were offered this service, it might constitute a WOW Moment. It is much easier to WOW a guest when expectations are lower. The three things that impact expectations are typically:

1. reason for visiting
2. price
3. market positioning

The guest who uses a hotel for a 'stopover' will typically choose a hotel that is relatively inexpensive and one that positions itself as a 'welcome stopover' or something along their requirements. They'll judge whether the way in which the hotel is presented aligns with their needs. In this case, the opportunity to WOW is huge, as it's likely that expectations will be nothing more than pleasant staff, clean sheets and a quiet night's sleep. When expectations are this low it opens up a world of opportunities for inexpensive WOW Moments that demonstrate the importance of the guest's stay.

Being able to measure the expectations of guests will largely come down to the way the hotel is presented. I'd argue that this is more important than price and purpose of stay. In fact, the market positioning will often denote purpose. If a hotel describes itself as 'luxury', guests will, oddly enough, expect luxury. The same is true for budget properties. Of course this is obvious, but the deeper and more significant point here is that in high-end hotels it's the experience that makes the stay. Not the stay that makes the experience.

Let me explain.

When you pay to visit a hotel that classes itself as 'luxury' you pay for the décor. The elaborate foyer. The Egyptian cotton sheets. The faultless marble floors. The landscaped gardens. The £5,000 armchair that resides by the elevators and never gets sat on. The unrequested biscotti that welcomingly arrives with your lattè. These are the physical elements that are required for classing and establishing the expectations. When you brand yourself with the L word, the service has to match too. That means there needs to be a complimentary newspaper of the guest's choice waiting on the doorstep. The room service needs to be swift. The reception phone needs to be answered within a few rings when a guest calls from their room. If these things are not in place then it's likely that the guest's needs and expectations will not be met and their experience will be underwhelming, despite their stay being comfortable and pleasant.

Similarly, guests at budget hotels expect less elaborate facilities, but also a very basic level of service; after all, most people agree that you get what you pay for. If a guest requests an international newspaper in a budget hotel they're unlikely to be given it and it's unlikely their experience will be ruined as a result. If the staff are pleasant but a little unhelpful, as is often the case in budget properties, the experience will unlikely be unaffected. When guests stay in a budget hotel, the stay is normally more important that the experience.

Whether a guest chooses to stay in a high-end property or a low-end one, one common theme is important across the board – value. Every hotel guest in the world wants value for money. They want to know that what they got was not only worth the money, but, for what they experienced they got a great deal. This is true for whether you pay £12 to sleep in a dorm room in a hostel, or whether you spend £12,000 a night in a top London hotel. Deliver a valuable experience and you'll achieve and exceed your guests' expectations.

The downside is that value is an intangible perception that will be different for every guest. I stopped in a small café for lunch with a few friends not long ago and the place was nothing fancy. Just your basic café that served good, honest food. One of the guys I was with complained about his meal. The rest of us sniggered at the thought that he was complaining in a small independent café. Our expectation was low. But my friend didn't feel as if he got value for the £4.35 that he spent on his jacket potato! The rest of us did. So this stuff will vary. That means that, as a hotelier, you have to work extremely hard to ensure that you are *over delivering* to meet your guests' value requirements.

The good news, however, is that value perception is very often not related to cost from your side of things. If a guest has spent £12,000 per night for their stay, it doesn't mean that £11,500 has to be spent on delivering sufficient value. But it will mean that the guest has to experience things that were not expected and that demonstrated genuine thought. An exceptionally pleasant and capable receptionist who quickly and efficiently handled a request from the guest to be moved from a twin room to a double room demonstrates value. A welcome note personally addressed to the guest perched on the beak of an origami swan towel, standing tall on the bed as the guest arrives, demonstrates value. The room service order that is received within a few minutes of it being ordered demonstrates value. These things are all free to do, by the way.

When you're able to deliver a sufficient amount of value for money on a consistent basis, that's when you can charge more. When you charge more, the importance of creating WOW Moments becomes more important because you must ensure that the expectations and the value perception is being met and exceeded. This book, if nothing else, provides an opportunity for you to implement WOW Moments that exceed guest expectations and deliver higher value in such a way that does not require huge expense and a great amount of resource.

Regardless of the level of service and quality of facilities that your hotel is known for, there are certain expectations that guests have come to expect. They expect to be welcomed into the property. They expect there to be someone to greet them at reception. They expect to be given a room key. They expect a good night's sleep. They expect clean and comfortable beds. The list goes on.

The real big wins are when you take those basic elements synonymous with decent service at any hotel that your guest has ever experienced, and tweak those procedures to deliver a unique and remarkable stay. Do that and you begin to surprise your guest. You start to deliver unexpected moments that (delivered correctly) will WOW them. This is why what you do before your guest arrives and after they leave matters so much. Engaging with your guest, with a personal message from the General Manager, using a communication method that the guest does not expect, prior to their formal arrival will be so powerful. The type of greeting they receive when they arrive is so important; make that bit special, demonstrate an exceptionally warm and heartfelt greeting that is unlike any other greeting that the guest has ever experienced and you will leave a great, lasting impression.

The top hotels get this. They know their guests typically frequent luxury hotels all over the world, and they do everything they can to make their experience unique. The Savoy, for example, does not have a reception per se. The doorman greets you and directs you to an area which is much more welcoming than a reception. They understand that in order to justify the price, and to realise their ambition to stay as one of the world's top hotels, they must offer something different. Something that their guests are not expecting that demonstrates value.

My advice is to not only get super clear on the experience you offer, but also spend a night at those hotels with whom you are in direct competition. Developing an understanding of your competitions' experience will allow you to mould your own experience into a more remarkable and differentiating one.

CHAPTER THREE

The Entire Guest Experience

Hotels are lucky. Few businesses have the opportunity to build a relationship with their customers to the same level as hotels do. Unfortunately few hotels take advantage of their privileged amount of exposure they have with their customers, or realise that they are one of the few businesses that have a really desirable product their customers love to buy. I'll happily spend £250 on a golf break for two days, but really dislike the £100 that comes out of my account to cover my accountancy bill each month!

When you think about it, there are really very few businesses whose product or service is so all-encompassing for a short burst of time. The strength of the relationship with your guests is the average of all of the touch points that you have with them. A touch point is simply a moment when your guest interacts or communicates with your hotel. The most notable touch point is often considered to be the reception greeting. This is hugely important as, in many cases, it will be the first time your guest has come face-to-face with someone who represents your hotel. However, it is not the first touch point. This is a mistake that all too many hotels make. The first touch point for a guest will be the booking process, if they booked directly through your website (in many cases it will also be the marketing messages which you have used in the first place, but this subject goes beyond what is covered in this book).

It's important to note here that the aim is to achieve that WOW before they get to the hotel; before they arrive and are greeted by the receptionist. Understandably, this might not always be feasible, particularly when a guest has booked a day or only a couple of days before they are due to stay, which is very often the case. Think about it like this: when you book a hotel you'll want to know, whether consciously or subconsciously, these three things:

1. That your booking is confirmed

Every time I walk into a hotel having made a booking through a major booking engine, I get this pang of 'I hope they have my booking confirmed'. Every time. Although the reality is that it is confirmed every time, I can't help thinking that something *may* have gone wrong. But is it because I'm a worrier, or is it because the hotel hasn't bothered to get in touch to let me know they've received my booking?

2. That you received value for money

Everyone loves a bargain. We all want to think we got an amazing deal whatever it is we buy. The fact is that hotel rooms have had to (in most cases) become so competitive that very few guests are paying the normal rate, but only when booking via a booking engine do I actually get told what amount or percentage I actually saved. This is a really powerful tool which, frankly, is just not used enough. Imagine when you next walk into a hotel as a guest, you're greeted by the friendly receptionist who confirms your stay and congratulates you for saving £25 off the normal rate for this room. How good would you feel?

3. That you didn't make the wrong choice.

Three significant points for you to consider here:

a) Your guest has been told they've saved money so they feel good about themselves that they chose to make this particular booking – you've just made a very positive start to building a powerful relationship with that guest

b) You've also told them how much they've saved so they now think, well, I've just been gifted £25 of disposable income – that's a few rounds, a bottle of bubbly, room service, a shoulder massage. Not everyone will think like that, but many will.

c) This point ties into the last one: it's about how the guest is made to feel as a result of being at your hotel. If the first, second and third touch points are met with unfriendliness, and from members of staff who quite clearly don't care all that much, this third point will be false and the guest will put blame on themselves, wondering why they ever bothered to book *this* hotel.

So the obvious thing to do is to ensure that the first touch point is to clarify these three things in your guest's mind before they've even set foot in the hotel. If you're serious about WOWing your customers, increasing their average spend and increasing repeat and referral bookings, then you really should be making sure that they're walking in with rose tinted glasses; that their first touch point has already WOWed them.

Remember that human beings like to categorise, as in the example in Chapter One with the happy and miserable baristas in the two coffee shops. The next time you walk in, talk about or even walk past the happy barista coffee shop, you'll have an affinity with it, you'll think good feelings and may even veer towards it despite not needing a coffee. It sounds silly but this sort of stuff happens *every day*. Similarly, the coffee shop with the miserable barista will evoke bad or negative feelings when you happen to stumble upon it, either in conversation or in person.

These principles apply if you've managed to WOW or disappoint your guest before they've set foot in your hotel. You want them walking in with the pre-arrival WOW, you want them walking in having already been impressed.

Think back to the last time you booked a doctor's appointment, dentist, hairdressers, beauty treatment etc. Anytime when you've booked an appointment for a service – even though doctors and dentists are different in often being an unpleasant experience – what happened with that experience? You booked and you went. You may have booked weeks or months in advance for a hairdresser's appointment. Did they get in touch to confirm? Did you receive a quick text that read something like this:

> Hi Sam, we've got you booked in tomorrow at 4pm. We look forward to seeing you then. All the best, Max, at Max's Salon.

Some services are great at this; most aren't. This text may seem insignificant, but not only has it confirmed and reminded the customer about the appointment, it has demonstrated that these guys are on the ball. These guys are going to look after me. These guys are looking forward to seeing me.

WOW Moment 1 – Confirmation Text

Now in most cases this isn't always a WOW because, whilst it's nice to receive, it's not necessarily unexpected. At the time of writing this book, I have never had a text like this from a hotel prior to my arrival. In most cases I would have spent over £100 on a hotel stay; typically these hotels will be four star and not one has sent a text which would have cost them no more than four pence! And yet the impact would have been WOW! Here's a good example of what I and every other guest that visits your hotel would like to receive:

> Dear Mr Jones. Here at Made-Up Hotel we were delighted to receive your booking to stay with us on DATE. Both I and my staff look forward to welcoming you into our hotel. If you require anything in the meantime, don't hesitate to get in touch. Yours most sincerely, Steven Smith, General Manager.

The point needs to be made here that, should you receive the booking via an OTA, you're unlikely to have all the guest's information, particularly their mobile phone number. Nonetheless, those that book with you direct should be required to punch it in when making the booking as it will quickly become a fantastic asset in delivering an experience that WOWs them.

WOW Moment 2 – Traffic Reports

There's even more opportunities to WOW when you open yourself up to the medium of text messages. Traffic reports. It might sound like a lot of work, but that couldn't be further from the truth. You'll need one member of staff to be responsible for this between the hours of 8am – 12pm. Sign them up to receive a text message from the local traffic report, and if there's been an incident on a major road that could affect the guest's journey, drop them a text. You'll have the phone numbers segregated by arrival date so everyone arriving on that date gets a text about tailbacks on the M40 by Junction 3 going northbound, for example.

For most of your guests this may be irrelevant, but that's not the point. The point is that regardless of whether they're arriving by train, from the other direction, or not until much later in the day, you will be demonstrating concern about their journey. That's a great WOW.

And what about the cost? Well, you'll be using an internet-based, bulk text service and won't be paying more than four pence per text message. Let's assume you have 100 guests staying in 60 rooms on a given day, and each room has been purchased for an average of £80 per night.

100 texts at £0.04 = £4

60 rooms at £80 = £4,800

£4 as a percentage of £4,800 is 0.08%

Invest £4 on this per day and you've already WOWed the 100 new arrivals on that day – it took five minutes and £4.

Here's what it might read like:

Dear Mr Jones. Steven here from Made Up Hotel. The Team and I are excited about welcoming you into the hotel later on today. If you're travelling by road to us, right now the M5 is a little slow southbound between J11A and J12 so you may wish to allow some extra time for your journey. Drive safely and see you shortly. Steven Smith, General Manager.

This brings us nicely onto the time when your guests check out and leave the hotel. Guess what, the experience isn't over! I would argue the 'days later' letter is the most important touch point of all; it's the last one, after all, and the one that will last longest – don't make it a bitter one! Now the days later letter is, as it sounds, simply a letter, sent a few days after the guest's stay. The content of this letter is crucial, though. You're looking for a WOW, and that means you are not doing any of the following:

- Asking for them to complete a short form about their stay
- Asking them if they could possibly tell their friends about the hotel
- Suggesting they book again soon, perhaps at a discount

You are just thanking them for coming to stay with you. I say this is the most powerful and important touch point for another reason; it's the one that they *really* don't expect because, in their mind, their experience has ended. Imagine how WOW their stay was with a dozen WOW Moments thrown in, they can't wait to get in front of their friends and tell them all about it, but before they've had the opportunity, they've been WOWed even *more* by a carefully written letter, signed from the General Manager, doing nothing more than thanking them for their custom and that they hoped they enjoyed their stay. Stop reading for 30 seconds and imagine how powerful that feeling will be from one of your guests, for your brand, for your business.

That's the feeling you're after.

Now, this isn't to say that you shouldn't ask your guests for feedback about their experience. Feedback will be invaluable to you if you take the time to read and review it. But remember that a WOW asks for nothing the guest doesn't really want to do. Asking your guest to venture to the bar for a free drink will be WOW, asking them to find a pen, write a few short sentences about their stay and post it back to you, or pop it in the feedback box before they leave will never, ever be a WOW. As soon as that thank you letter asks for feedback, it enters into the void of nothingness. You won't necessarily blemish your guest's overall experience but it will do nothing to enhance it.

I mentioned avoiding leaving that 'bitter taste' on your last touch point with your guest. Well you can take this quite literally if you like. Pop a little box of chocolates in with your thank you letter. It doesn't have to be a full box, in fact it shouldn't be, just four little bite-sized gourmet chocolates. This WOW will take full pride of place at the dinner party; it'll be the one thing that everyone remembers. It might even prompt a phone call to a friend: 'Sarah, you'll never guess what I received from that lovely hotel I stayed in last week...'

If you're laughing at this, you clearly don't know my mother. She will gossip on the phone to her sisters for hours, and anything demonstrating a real welcome gesture for her custom will have her on the phone to my Auntie Joyce immediately. My enthusiastic relatives aren't alone, and if your guests are middle-aged affluent women like my mum, it can happen to your hotel too. So get over how it sounds; this kind of thing can happen and if you're in the hotel business and care about providing an amazing experience and growing your business, this is the kind of reaction you should be aiming for.

WOW Moment 3 – Thank You Letter With Chocolates

There are three factors that will impact the effectiveness of this WOW:

1. Content – what you say to your guest
2. Appearance and quality: does it scream WOW?
3. Timeliness – when it arrives

Broadly speaking, you'll want to say these following things:

- *Thank you*
- *We hoped they enjoyed their stay*
- *If not, we'll want to put that right*
- *All the best*

It doesn't need to be an essay; go for quality over quantity. Here's a template that works well, feel free to use and WOW.

> *Dear Mrs Windsor,*
>
> *Myself and the team here at Made Up Hotel are absolutely delighted to have had you stay with us. I do hope your stay was enjoyable and we exceeded your expectations. If for whatever reason it wasn't, we'll be wanting to put that right; just pick up the phone and tell us about it on telephone number.....*
>
> *All the very best and thank you again for choosing Made Up Hotel.*
>
> *Yours sincerely,*
>
> *Adam N Hamadache*
> *General Manager*
>
> *PS. I hope you enjoy the chocolates, they are my personal favourites.*

In terms of quality, you'll want the letter to reflect your hotel well: if your hotel is the most beautiful country manor house, somehow a white DL envelope won't do it justice. Similarly, if you're a boutique, chic town house hotel, wax stamps won't really reflect the modernity of your establishment. Ultimately, you'll want to avoid this letter looking like every other bill and junk mail, so experiment with coloured envelopes, ribbons – anything that's going to stand out and make your hotel look great.

FREE DOWNLOAD

To download all the templates used in this book, and for a selection of my preferred suppliers, please visit www.wowguest.com/resources

In terms of timing, a second class stamp (or equivalent) sent on the day they leave the hotel will do the trick. This will mean that they'll receive it two to three days after their stay, a short enough time for the experience to be fresh in their minds, but long enough for the impact of this WOW to be met with welcome surprise.

WOW Moment 4 – Thank You / Feedback Call

To add even more weight to the Thank You Letter explained above, follow it up with a phone call a few days later. You may think that a thank you letter and a thank you phone call is a little over the top, but there's a very specific reason for it. You see, after they've been WOWed by the experience, after they've been WOWed further by the thank you letter whilst enjoying those delicious chocolates, you speak with them on the phone and ask whether you served them well. There's a golden rule here – nobody likes completing a survey but most people will gladly give you their opinion in a conversation. So once you've listened attentively to why their experience was so amazing for a few minutes, now's the time to ask politely if they wouldn't mind writing a few words on Trip Advisor. Believe me, if you've done your job well up to this point, most guests will be so grateful for all the WOW Moments they received, including the phone call they've just received, that they'll be delighted to help out.

Just to clarify – doing this with every guest is unlikely to be feasible. But I'll bet if you make one phone call a day, allocating no more than 15 minutes a day for three months, you'll be likely to receive approximately 50 excellent reviews on Trip Advisor.

What would 50 Excellent reviews do to your Trip Advisor page ranking?

What would that mean to your hotel in terms of extra bookings (remembering that nearly half of guests thinking about booking at your hotel check out your Trip Advisor Page before making their decision)?

Last question: Is that worth 15 minutes of your day?

Good. Get your diary out and block out 15 minutes for a conversation today.

CHAPTER FOUR

THINK ABOUT YOUR OVERHEADS IN A NEW WAY

You will have read quite a bit by now about how much of an impact a WOW Moment can have on your guest's experience. You may be thinking it all sounds very nice and in an ideal world you'd be doing all sorts of things to make their experience a WOW one, but doesn't it all sound a little expensive and a waste of money?

No. No. No. If you've fallen into that train of thought, get out of it now because WOWs don't have to cost the earth, nor are they a waste of time if implemented properly. The cost of a moment that WOWs will vary. Some are completely free, but they require a little training and patience.

Some WOWs do carry a significant cost: integrating your database into your phone system so everyone who has ever stayed with you was presented to your member of staff on speed dial, would be costly, but consider this for a few minutes:

Mrs Jones last stayed with you nine months ago, she's gone quiet, but randomly she calls, perhaps to enquire about a room next week. Now imagine the receptionist answers the phone as follows:

"Good afternoon, Made Up Hotel, Jessica speaking, how are you today, Mrs Jones?"

"Oh, err, hello, how did you know it was me?"

"You're an important guest of ours, Mrs Jones, we like to keep your details on file so we can serve you as best we can the next time you stay with us."

Now Mrs Jones just wanted to check availability. She's trying a few hotels around the area, but after that greeting I would say that in most cases, price would have become secondary; she would have been so impressed with that WOW Moment, she'd have booked there and then.

The reality is that most WOW Moments don't cost much, certainly not compared to how much your guest will be spending with you throughout the duration of their stay. Here's a working example of a WOW Moment that I advise all of my clients to do: it is so perfectly simple, yet I have never, ever seen it done without my recommendation. When you think about what you want to achieve as a hotel, your answer should almost certainly be to provide an amazing customer experience and to encourage your guests to spend more with you. If you ignore every other WOW Moment in this book, implement this one *today*.

WOW Moment 5 – Text Offering Free Drink At The Bar

Text again. It's such a powerful and underused medium to communicate with your guests. No medium is so immediate and has such a high read rate. If you're getting 25% of your warm email list to read each email you send in its entirety, you are doing very well. Text messages to guests, when they're staying in your hotel, will be read 99% of the time. The 1% typically have run out of battery!

But I digress. You're texting them and offering them a free drink at the bar on you. Whaaaaaaaaat?! I hear your inner voice cry, too much to give away; we'll lose money; think about the lost margins… Forget all this nonsense. Say it out loud:

It's nonsense.

Now imagine that feeling of pure WOW when Jessica and Kevin, celebrating their 40th wedding anniversary at your hotel, have just received an invitation to each have a free drink at the bar. WOW.

So let's do some number crunching to support this. Let's say you have 500 guests stay with you in a week. Let's also assume that 25% take up your kind offer of a free drink at the bar (this is high, by the way).

500 x 25% = 125 guests have one free drink per week

Let's also say for round numbers, that the hard cost to the hotel of a glass of wine, beer, spirit and mixer etc is £1.

Hard cost to hotel per week: £125

Hard cost to hotel per year = £125 x 52 = £6,500

Whether your guests take you up on this rather generous offer or not, a WOW will have been achieved. It just cost you 25p to achieve that WOW.

The fundamental point when it comes to the financial implications of your WOWs is to understand, and fully understand, the hard cost to your business. Never think of a cost in isolation. If I tell you that to take part in our six-month Training Course the fee will be £100,000, (it's considerably less if you were wondering) the incorrect response would be to fall off your chair, have a heart attack, come out in a cold sweat or all of the above! Such is the tendency when we hear a large amount of money that we may have to pay. The correct response is to ask the question, 'Compared to what?' If that £100,000 investment brought in £200,000 in extra sales as a direct result of the work, would you consider that a good investment? Perhaps you're in the mindset that 100% return is not a sufficiently high return to be worth your while. I can't tell you what the minimum return should be – only you will know that. Let's, though, think of it this way: if you had a machine in your office – let's assume it's in place of the coffee machine – And every time you wandered over to this machine you put a £1 coin in, you pressed a button which wasn't too much effort, and out popped two £1 coins, wouldn't you be on it all day every day? Wouldn't you feed it more and more money? Why? Because it's been proven to work.

These machines exist in business. They just don't sit in your office and it's not always as simple as walking over to it, inserting a £1 coin and pressing a button. My point is: find your money machine. You do that by testing, measuring, testing, measuring, testing, measuring... you get the point. If you've been reading this book and liking the ideas, try them, now. Stop what you're doing, implement one of my WOW Moments and trial it for a month. Be resourceful, find a small amount of cash to invest and test it for a month. The reality is that the things I'm talking about in this book work in most cases, when implemented correctly. These WOW Moments are your very own money machine, *if* and it's a big if, you are prepared to do a little more work than walking over to a machine and pressing a button. Do the hard work; do the heavy lifting to get the machine into your hotel; make sure it works and, as soon as you've got it nailed, I guarantee it will be even easier than walking over and pressing a button. It will work on its own.

Going back to *WOW Moment 5: offering a free drink via text to every guest.* Let's dive into the numbers a little further and understand its potential as a sales driver. To reiterate, we've acknowledged that the hard cost of the free drink is £1 and that the response rate is 25% over a typical period. Also, that the hard cost to the hotel over a 12 month period will be £6,500. In a 12 month period, we will see 6,500 guests enjoy a free drink. Now let's assume that the average cost for a drink is £5.

Typically, over time, the following should start to happen:

20% buy 1 more drink at £5 = £6,500
10% buy 2 more drinks at £5 = £3,250
4% buy 3 more drinks at £5 = £1,300

2% buy 4 more drinks at £5 = £650

1% buy 5+ more drinks at £5 = £325

This totals £12,025 in additional revenue over a year.

For the purposes of understanding the profit potential, we'll deduct the original £6,500, which was the hard cost of the free drink to all that came. We'll also take into account that each text cost 4 pence too:

500 guests per week x 52 weeks in a year x 4 pence per text = £1,040

That's 12,025 – 6,500 – 1,040 = £4,485 net profit

To clarify, you have put £7,540 in your free drink text money machine and you've got £12,025 out of it. That means for every £1 you've put into it, you've received approximately £1.59 out of it. But most crucially, you have achieved the following:

- Created tens of thousands of WOW Moments that will manifest themselves into dinner party anecdotes, friend referrals and positive reviews
- Created an additional revenue stream and increased your guests' average spend

- You have done the work upfront, measured, tweaked and created a system that works with minimal ongoing effort

Now, when your hotel is implementing a whole series of WOW Moments think about the potential first, from a customer experience perspective and second, from a profit perspective, and the potential to achieve great things really can increase exponentially.

CHAPTER FIVE

Encourage Your Guests To Get More Than A Bed

I've touched upon some of the forms of communication that you can use to WOW your guests, text being, I think, the most immediate and effective. The beauty about these WOW Moments is that the medium in which a piece of information is delivered can very often be the WOW. And it needn't be expensive, as with the text message: using a bulk text message service, you'd be looking at 4 pence per text. It doesn't have to be anything new, either. Think about all the literature you make available for your guests when they arrive in their room. Typically, they will include some sort of welcome letter, room service menu, hotel guide about all of the facilities they can make use of, etc. It doesn't matter how many hotels I stay in, whether I'm there for business or pleasure, I seem to always dive straight into this literature, normally to find out what time the pool is open until, what time breakfast is, etc. I'm not suggesting that every guest of yours reads the leaflets and pamphlets that you make available in the room, but my research certainly suggests most do. This touch point is crying out for a WOW.

How? Well it's really quite simple, this one. Make it personal. The unexpected forms of communication that are personal to the individual guest and show a level of thoughtfulness will be more effective and also produce that WOW Moment that we're going for.

Two great ways in which you can WOW on arrival – I suggest you use both:

WOW Moment 6 – Welcome Letter Handed On Arrival

Your guest approaches the reception to check in. They hand over a credit card perhaps, the receptionist hands over the key and tells the guest where to find their room. On the most basic level, this is what happens. The next few sentences may sound silly to the cynics reading this, but this is a really important part in the guest's stay because it is the first physical touch point.

They have been handed a key and it'll be the first time they handle anything that's associated with the hotel. In 99 out of 100 cases this will just be 'good' and won't be given a second thought. However, imagine for a second that the key was disgustingly dirty, like it had been traipsed through the mud before you gave it to your guest; in this instance the relationship between hotel and guest has got off to terrible start – and what must they be expecting when they enter their room?

On the other hand, imagine that when the receptionist hands over the room key, she does so with a smile, along with a high quality envelope sealed with a wax stamp, addressed to Mr Hamadache. Well, I'd feel rather special, wouldn't you?

Inside is a letter that reads something like this:

Dear Mr Hamadache,

Welcome to Made Up Hotel. We are delighted to have you stay with us and will do everything possible to make your stay with us as comfortable as possible. My name is Steven and I'm the General Manager here; if

I'm not around, you'll find my colleagues, June and David, here to help.

I see that you'll be joining us for breakfast tomorrow morning: we pride ourselves on the level of choice we offer so I'm sure you'll find something to your taste. We serve breakfast at 6.30am until 10am. If you need to be up and out a little earlier, no problem, just let us know and we'll have our chefs prepare you something.

You might also like to take advantage of our award-winning gym, spa and swimming pool facilities whilst you're here. You can do so anytime daily between 7am and 10pm. Forgotten your swimming costume? Not a problem, our gym shop is open between 8am and 8pm, should you wish to visit.

All of the additional information you'll find within the welcome pack, laid out for you on your bed; please feel free to read at your leisure.

If you need anything else at all from us, including room service or taxis, just hit zero on your telephone, and you'll be put through to either Sandra or Jessica on reception.

The team and I would like to extend our warmest of welcomes to you and wish you a pleasant stay.

Yours sincerely

SIGNATURE
Steven Mayfield
General Manager

WOW. A few points worth noting about this – I can count on one hand how many times I have received a letter like this from a hotel; none have been written with the guest in mind like this, and yet it's the simplest thing. Please note that at no point is Steven selling to me. He is simply informing me of the facilities and the times everything is available. If you gave this letter to every guest over the course of the year, would you expect swimming costume sales to go up? I would; perhaps not dramatically, but I'd expect to a small percentage to resonate with that one sentence, 'Forgotten your swimming costume?' Try it: measure it, tweak it, measure it. You might find a four figure increase to your swimming costume sales.

WOW Moment 7 – Arrival Text

Your guest has been handed this beautifully crafted letter, they've navigated their way to their room and now they're sitting on the bed being WOWed by the letter. Give it an hour or so, then drop them a text that reads as follows:

> Hi Mr Hamadache, Steven the GM here. I trust you found your room ok and everything has met your expectation so far. Let us know if there's anything we can do for you – you can reply to this text or dial zero on your room telephone. Enjoy your stay.

This is great on so many levels:

1. It's personal – *Hi Mr Hamadache*

2. It's familiar – *Steven the GM here.* You've just read a letter from Steven so you know who he is (and trust me, if you make that letter as beautifully presented as you can, addressed directly to the guest, every guest will open it up and have a read!).

3. It's thoughtful – *I trust you found your room ok*

4. It encourages queries and sales – *Let us know if there's anything we can do for you. You can reply to this text or dial zero on your room telephone.* (Send this message out in bulk to everyone who has arrived in the last couple of hours and see how many texts and calls to reception you get as a result. It might not be many, but I guarantee that over the course of a month, or a year, you'll be receiving all sorts of orders that you otherwise wouldn't).

I've talked at some length about offering a free drink at the bar via text. This is effective because it's an incentive to get you down to the bar. Obvious, right? Carefully controlled offers and incentives should be used as common practice to encourage use of your most profitable facilities. In most cases these will likely be your restaurant, bar, room service, beauty and massage services, etc. Let's use restaurant as an example for how you can successfully drive more income whilst ensuring your focus is always on the customer experience.

I still see restaurants offering 10% off as an incentive to visit. If you are still doing this in your restaurant, stop it now – the world has moved on and it frankly doesn't excite anyone anymore. Since the financial crash of 2008, promotional marketing has advanced into its own discipline and consumers are much more savvy when it comes to any sort of offers, particularly when it comes to dining. Pizza Express pioneered the paper voucher for BOGOF pizza any day of the week; Groupon introduced us to the daily deal where we were constantly being told how much we were saving despite spending more on things we didn't need or in many cases use.

At a slight tangent, amazingly many daily deals website's biggest revenue comes from all of the deals that never get used: they keep 100% of the money until a voucher is redeemed. And the amount of vouchers that never get used is quite alarming.

I digress. The point here is that the way we dine has changed. And if your restaurant isn't turning over what it should, you need to pay attention.

On another issue, if your restaurant is full every night and you don't need to discount, that's fine too. Some restaurants just have sufficient demand particularly if situated in a busy urban location and importantly the restaurant has its own street entrance. But I suspect for most, the answer to the following question – could I make more money out of my restaurant? – is 'Yes'.

So what to do? As a general rule, no one is getting out of bed for less than 25%, often quite literally, in our industry. But how you dress it up and market it really is key. A nice way of doing this is to make it exclusive, only to your guests, and make sure you shout about how exclusive it is. The second way is to make a big deal of it. Go back to that welcome letter from the GM; he could have offered 25% off in the restaurant at any point during your stay – a short sentence which is likely to have got a little lost. Or there could have been a beautifully presented £10/£20/£30-off gift voucher within the letter, in shiny silver or gold, explaining that the guest need only to head down to the restaurant to redeem. This, to clarify, is not expensive when bought in bulk – a few hundred pounds. If you're worried about cost, put your prices up 10% or 20% whilst adding some extra value.

The key to anything is to measure response. Would this be a WOW? Technically, no as it's selling, but it's still an unexpected, beautifully presented gesture that is offering your guest something of value whilst encouraging them to spend more and gain more from their stay. Sounds good to me.

So we've used the example of the restaurant, which is usually the easier of the upsells, seeing as everyone has to eat! Encouraging your guests to use more of your 'luxury upsells' will be more difficult. These are things like your massage and beauty treatments, room service etc. Nonetheless, a carefully implemented and marketed sales widget will often give you the response you desire. A sales widget is effectively a package, a bundle of services grouped together with a high perceived value.

Remember that your guests are constantly looking for an opportunity to make the most of their stay, particularly for leisure guests, but true for business guests as well. Your guests are also looking for value. Something they can tell their friends about – everyone loves a bargain!

When considering what services to bundle up, it's worth thinking about the types of stay that your guests are on. Is it an anniversary getaway? Birthday? Have they come away to rekindle their love after a turbulent few months? Is it a lads' weekend away? Girls' weekend away? This is hugely important when you come not only to packaging, but also to naming the sales widget. You'll know the type of guest and the types of stay that typically occurs within your hotel – make sure you target.

Think of it like this: a couple have come away on an anniversary, a young couple, married for two years, no kids at home, just looking for a getaway and to spend some quality time with each other. When they arrive in their room, there's a leaflet offering them the opportunity to take advantage of the *Special Anniversary Package* – ideal for couples wanting that extra special something from their stay. It might include:

- His and hers full body massage
- Followed by Champagne afternoon tea
- Champagne, strawberries and dipping chocolate waiting for them in their room
- Rose petals scattered on the bed

You get the picture. Individually these elements might come to £250, in which you still receive quite a hefty margin. Package that up as one – you might decide to discount, you might not. The key is to test and measure. I've had this sort of weekend with a partner and would almost certainly have taken advantage of it, because it was aimed so tightly at me. What I didn't do, and almost certainly wouldn't do and neither will the majority of your guests, is to personally pop down to the spa and order two massages, go into the restaurant and order two Champagne afternoon teas, before asking for a bottle of Champagne to be sent up to the room. I'm not saying this doesn't happen, but look what's happening here: transaction after transaction after transaction. It feels like you're spending an awful lot of money, splashing out every couple of hours for the next big gesture, when really what I want to make this stay really worthwhile is to simply pay for something that encompasses a great number of things, sit back and enjoy.

Don't stop with just one package. Broadly speaking, 20% of your guests will spend more with you if you give them the opportunity to buy what they want.

I'll say that again so it sinks in: broadly speaking, 20% of your guests will spend more with you if you give them the opportunity to buy what they want.

That means that if you're making an anniversary or a birthday package available, or whatever occasion is relevant to your hotel, you might have one at £50, one at £100 and the very premium at £250, for example.

The trick is to really understand your guests and what they want. It will be subtly different for each guest, but the likelihood is that most guests will fall in to a small number of categories. Make sure you know what they are.

Just to re-emphasise this point, because it was one of my very first lessons in business: everything you sell should have a standard, bronze, silver and gold (there is also a fairly strong argument for having a platinum as well). Odds are, you're already doing this with standard and premium rooms and suites if you have them. This should be no different for almost everything you sell.

When you go into Starbucks to buy a coffee, it's no coincidence that you've got three size options. I visited a safari park in Woburn, Bedfordshire not long ago and tickets were £25 but they were also selling £75 VIP safari tickets where you get chauffeured around and get closer to the animals – very smart indeed.

If you've ever been to a posh cocktail bar and looked at the sparkling wine list, you'll often see a magnum of Cristal at some ludicrous price – it's not there to show off, it's there because the owners of that bar are savvy enough to understand that this will be exactly what a small percentage of their customers will want or can afford. Ironically, anyone who buys it is almost certainly buying it to show off! Make sure that you are making a premium product available and you might be surprised at just how willing some of your guests are to part with £500 for the most premium offering you can muster. Then sit back and applaud yourself on what a remarkable business decision you made when you sell 10 in three months and just added £5k to the business for next to no extra work. Try it now.

We've discussed sales widgets, offers and incentives, which should be fairly exciting prospects to increase revenue from guests staying in the hotel. Now I want to talk about something that is arguably the most important of the lot. Guarantees. Have the courage and belief to guarantee your services. And just to prove that I practice what I preach, I should mention that all of The Wow Guest Group's services, including our 21 Week Training Course is 100% Guaranteed. Offer your guests their money back if they're not completely satisfied. If you're not currently doing this, you're probably falling into small thinking territory: what if everyone claims they weren't satisfied? They won't. What if half the people claim their money back? Trust me, they won't. What if some claim their money back? They will and it's important that they do. Bear with me on this…

A guarantee reverses the risk. When you've presented a guest with an upsell option worth, say, £100 in, let's say, the form of a relaxing package sales widget, the guest hasn't budgeted for it and they're not sure whether to do it or not. If you've guaranteed that widget, they'll feel more relaxed about doing it; in many cases that guarantee will be the gentle prod that moves them from a contemplator to a buyer.

Now some will claim, of course they will. But this is where testing and measuring becomes more important than ever. If you launch a sales widget, trial for two months and in that time you get 30 orders, you are happy with the return, but it's one every couple of days and you think it could do better. In the next two months you alter your marketing materials to offer a guarantee. During that period you sell 50, but five people claim on the guarantee. Well, the guarantee has just brought in 15 more sales (and the hard cost of the sales widgets that were claimed against of course). Just by altering your marketing material to reverse the risk, you increased your sales by 30%!

A tip here is that you don't want to be making the guarantee all that easy to claim. If it's as simple as approaching the reception and asking for your money back, it doesn't make sense. If the guarantee required the guest to write a letter to the General Manager explaining why they were not satisfied, somehow it doesn't seem so easy, but it shouldn't deter those with a genuine complaint about the service. Testing and measuring is crucial to be able to evaluate the success of a guarantee.

WOW Moment 8 – Romantic Gesture Offering

This one carries on from some of the topics discussed in this chapter. It's about offering a sales widget that will have your guests think, 'That's for me!' Many hotels that I work with and speak with offer some sort of romantic gesture service whereby they can pre-order roses, Champagne, rose petals on the bed, etc. to be displayed and ready for them when they arrive. It's a very neat way of upselling and provides a genuinely valuable service for the guest who wishes to surprise their partner with a romantic gesture. What many fail to do is to offer that service when in the hotel. Why? This is bonkers. Some men (and some women) would bite your arm off if you gave them the opportunity to WOW their partner with minimal hassle or effort from them.

So give them the opportunity! Display an ad in the gents' and women's toilets and changing rooms, offering them a series of romantic gesture packages that might include:

- Rose petals on the bed
- Flowers in the room

- Origami kissing swans fashioned from towels displayed on the bed
- Champagne
- Strawberries
- Chocolates

Make it easy for them to buy: offer a phone number and even a text service; implement the service at a time when they're not in the room and the guest has the pleasure of watching his/her partner's face when they re-enter their room and the room has been dressed so beautifully and romantically.

I love this WOW Moment because it allows your guest to WOW their partner. You are making a profitable service available whilst giving a handful of guests *exactly* what they want from their stay.

You can find a list of companies and resources on www.wowguest.com/resources

CHAPTER SIX

Your Guest's Experience Extends Beyond Your Walls

When guests come to stay at your hotel, the likelihood is that they have come to see the locality within which you are situated. Not all, but in most cases this is true. Well if you are truly invested in making their experience as strong and as WOW as possible, you must acknowledge and accept that the whole experience matters to your guests. The last thing you want is for your guests to come away and say, 'The hotel was lovely, they really looked after us, but we didn't find all that much to do in Bath.' That sort of conversation is never going to get their friends excited about coming to stay with you. Now, of course you only have a small amount of control over their experience within the town, city or local area in which you are based and you can't control everything, but there's plenty you can be doing to facilitate an amazing experience and importantly to demonstrate that you care about their experience as a whole. An important thing to do here is to set up strategic partnerships with other businesses, such as local attractions, restaurants, bars, nightclubs, if they're appropriate to your type of clientele.

These strategic partnerships will ideally take the form of discounts and offers, exclusive to guests at your hotel. It might be a 25% discount on the pedalos which are popular on the lake in the summer; half price mini golf, two for one cocktails at a bar in town; kids eat free at a local pub.

The beauty of simply offering an exclusive discount is that a) you are referring business to these other local businesses so they should be happy to work with you, and b) you are not recommending, you are simply offering them the opportunity to experience the local amenities for less. Therefore, if your guests have an unsavoury experience it shouldn't impact on their perception of your hotel or their experience with you. I can't stress enough that this should be avoided at all costs, but I like to view it as a damage limitation exercise.

Guests like tangible things. So if you've done the hard work; been out and created strategic partnerships with some local businesses, it will be a little wasted if the only way it's passed onto your guests is by the receptionist simply telling your guests that they can save X% at so-and-so. A good way to make this effort tangible, memorable and more impactful is to create a coupon booklet. Now it doesn't have to be an inch thick and full of useless stuff that your guests will never use, but it should be a handful of perforated coupons that will offer your guests some decent money off on an exclusive basis. Exclusive means that you have gone out of your way to make their experience better value. Only by being a customer of yours can they get *this* service at *that* price. You'll want to make sure this is hammered home because the WOW Moment is in the effort you've gone to and the service that you've made available to them, not whether they use the service or not.

If your property is particularly boutique, traditional or otherwise luxurious, the concept of a coupon booklet may be a little unsuitable for the brand and the types of clientele you cater for. A more suitable way of manifesting these exclusive offers might be online, behind a login wall in your website or simply e-mailed across. The point here is that you'll know what is suitable for your guests; the aim is to demonstrate that you have given some thought and care to their *entire* experience.

Similar to exclusive offers at local businesses, you should also be keeping abreast of which businesses are getting the best reviews in your local area. Remember you have a vested interest in your guests' entire experience. The underlying point of this entire book is that your current and previous guests are your lowest hanging fruit; they are your best source of repeat and referral bookings and, in most instances, the cost of acquiring these repeat and referral bookings will be far, far less than the cost of acquiring a new customer. This aside, if you are not keeping up to date with the local business reviews, chances are you're sending your guests off to an underwhelming experience. Similarly, if you can advise based on recent reviews, your guests will be thankful and appreciate this unexpected WOW Moment that you've just made available for them.

Trip Advisor and Urban Spoon are great for restaurant reviews. A good idea is, at the start of every month, print out the top-performing restaurants and some of the reviews that users have shared. Any awards that that local businesses have recently won is also a good thing to keep abreast of. Now you may decide to pop this on reception so guests can read as they're checking in; you might pop it in some kind of welcome pack (think back to *WOW Moment 6 – the welcome letter from GM*). I would also suggest you brief your receptionists about sharing which restaurants are good to eat at, their favourite, etc. It will offer a more personal touch to your guests.

Now you may be reading this and thinking, I have a restaurant (or several) within the hotel, why on earth would I want to send them out of the hotel to spend elsewhere? The answer is really quite simple. Because you should be investing in your guest's entire experience and not just trying to squeeze every penny you can out of them. The reality is that each hotel's situation, location, type of stay, etc. will differ, but in the majority of cases your hotel is not a suitable place for your guests to spend their entire stay. If you're a resort in the middle of nowhere, it might be; if you've got several different restaurants it may also be. But most hotels have one restaurant and perhaps a café or bistro. The point is that you have to be smart about what you're suggesting to your guests. For example, if you have a great Italian restaurant I'd strongly suggest not providing reviews for other Italians within the area, but there may be an incredible Indian restaurant down the road that you're more than happy to promote. Similarly, if your hotel has been getting some wonderful reviews ensure that your hotel is always at the top of that list. It might be that your restaurant is specifically designed for a fine dining-type diner where you're not getting much change from £20 for a starter. Well this is great, but there's nothing wrong with suggesting a good quality cheap eat place for a quick bite down the road if the reviews of that place are good.

What you're doing is building *trust*. It's so fundamentally important when building your relationship with your guest. Think about it like this: if all you're doing is recommending your own restaurant or bar, those which have a direct impact on your profit, then the trust isn't going to be all that strong. If, on the other hand, you are recommending places that you think your guests will enjoy, despite the fact they could spend their cash in your restaurant or your bar, that's hugely powerful. It will demonstrate to your guests that their experience is more important than your bottom line. The reality is that over time, if you get the experience right, your bottom line will also improve; every WOW Moment has been created with this in mind.

There is a third and final aspect worthy of discussion when it comes to your guests spending some time of their experience outside your walls. It has to do with referral fees. A referral fee may occur when you have created a strategic partnership with some other local businesses, or even national businesses: if you successfully refer a customer to them, you receive some form of commission from the sale. My view is very plain and simple on this: don't do it. There are obvious benefits from referring and recommending guests to businesses where you have a vested interest, but typically the revenue potential will be small and will come at a cost higher than you can afford. It will cost you, or at least damage your credibility, and fundamentally will do nothing for building that all important *trust* with your guests. If you are profiting from referring your guests to places, all of sudden your recommendation doesn't mean as much. Plus, the last thing you want to be doing is recommending your guests to visit places where the service or product is not up to scratch. On the other hand, if you are quite open about the fact that you do not profit from your recommendations, that in fact you simply recommend and advise based on the quality of previous guests' experience, this will be a fantastic way of building that all important trust.

WOW Moment 9 – Incentivising Staff To Ask About Guests' Experience In Local Places

The next thing to do is to have a system in place that will allow you to measure the experience that your guests have received at businesses outside of your hotel. This 'system' could be as simple as briefing your staff to ask what the guests have done that day; where did they go; where did they eat; did they enjoy it; would they recommend it to others? Then at the end of the week, have your staff email you with a summary of those conversations they have had. It might be as simple as 'The Red Lion – couple loved it'. Offer an incentive for the member of staff who has had the most conversations with guests that week. All of sudden, you have a hotel full of staff who are showing a genuine interest in their guests' overall experience and you are receiving constant feedback about what's good and what's not.

A few months ago I stayed in a five star hotel in Dubai. I simply could not fault the service, other than the fact that none of my WOW Moments were in place! But beyond that all of the elements were in place to make our experience as comfortable and as enjoyable as possible. On the day we were leaving we headed outside to grab a taxi. There was a shopping centre with a taxi rank across the road from the hotel, but one of the doormen asked if we'd like him to hail us a taxi. We thought, why not? Now it was the last day of the holiday so we only had a little bit of the local currency left and I knew what a cab cost to the airport as we'd already done the journey once, although from a standard rank taxi. The doorman hailed a cab, an unmarked Mercedes pulled up and he began putting our bags in the back. Without thinking, we jumped in the back and, just before he pulled away, the doorman spoke to the driver and told him a price to charge us. It was double that of a normal cab! I asked the driver about the price and he explained that his taxi company worked with the hotel and split the extended revenue. I was furious and so disappointed. If it was a long drive to the airport and we had specified that we wanted to travel in a little more comfort, then this luxurious Mercedes would have been ideal and I would have been happy to pay the premium. The reality was that the airport was 20 minutes away and I felt that this was a last ditch attempt to squeeze the last penny out of their guests by encouraging them to use this unwanted premium service. It was completely unwarranted, just so they could add an additional revenue stream to their bottom line. What a bitter taste left from what was otherwise a remarkable experience. Two things stay with me from that stay:

1. I won't be going back
2. I won't be recommending that friends stay there

But at least they made an extra £7 from me in that commission!

WOW Moment 10 – Build A Portfolio Of Guest Reviews

Reviews are important; they can be incredibly influential in buying decisions and also taken with a pinch of salt. Websites like Trip Advisor are a selection of comments and opinions made by strangers we'll never meet, or have any interest in meeting. But what a wonderfully simple service that many have a great affiliation to. A fantastic WOW Moment that can be implemented today is to start building your very own in-house review board. Have your staff ask your guests about where they've been outside of the hotel, did they enjoy it, would they recommend it etc. This in itself is a powerful tool because you're showing an interest in your guests' stay. Second thing: let those guests know they can leave a review so you can ensure you are advising other guests on local businesses to visit based on a recent guest's experience. You'll quickly find that many guests will be more than happy to share.

Lastly, once you've begun building up a few reviews, share them with your guests. This could be in many formats, but I would suggest simply pinning to the wall near reception and perhaps even sending a text message informing guests that it's there. Have it read, *'Here's what our guests say about X'*

You can make this even more powerful by adding names, pictures and date of stay of the reviewing guests. You may even choose to have a tablet computer at reception where guests can jump on and leave their review. You might like to have a restaurant of the week review board. And whilst you're at it, ask your guests who have dined in your in-house restaurant or enjoyed a drink at your bar, to share. What's great about this is that you're not selling it yourself, you're letting your former happy guests sell it for you. Trial for a month, measure your like-for-like sales from the previous year and see if there's a notable increase. That should all take you no more than 10-15 minutes a week and you've squeezed a few strong WOWs in there as well. Well done you!

CHAPTER SEVEN

A Bad Experience Is Just Another Opportunity To WOW

This may be the most useful information I can give you: even the most exquisite, expertly run hotels in the world get complaints, give bad experiences and have things that shouldn't go wrong go wrong. The smart hotels, however, know what to do when it happens – which it will from time to time. In short, the way in which your hotel as a collective handles a bad experience will demonstrate just how important your guests' stay is to you. And by now you'll know that your guests' experience must, absolutely must, be at the very core of your business.

Things will happen that will affect the experience that you want your guests to have. It might be rude staff, it might be a mismanaged booking, it might be that the waitress spilt coffee all down a lady's beautiful new white dress. This stuff happens and you had better be prepared for when it does. Depending on the severity of the misdemeanour, you'll need to act accordingly to not only preserve the experience but in fact come out on the other side and turn it into a WOW. As a default plan, you'll always want to keep abreast of the occupancy in your higher priced rooms; it might be a suite, a sea view room, or simply a bigger room. A free upgrade is a very powerful thing because it is a low (if not no) cost gesture to you, but has a very high value to your guest. Now, it might not always be needed. If you have received a complaint from a guest that a member of staff was abrupt or rude, you will be surprised, by simply giving your time and effort to the issue as quickly as possible as the General Manager, how powerful this is. If you are able to send a text message or make a phone call to that guest within a short time of the complaint arising, that's a WOW Moment. Go further by offering the most suitable form of compensation possible. If it's coffee on a dress, offer to take it to the dry cleaners. If it's rude staff, assess the issue and offer free drink in the bar, free room upgrade or complimentary spa treatment – all low cost/high value gestures.

Once the initial gesture has been made, compensation offered and taken, check in with that guest as often as is appropriate. Text message is the most suitable here as it's quick, unobtrusive and unexpected. But believe me, your guests will thank you for it.

Failing to handle a complaint or bad experience with a WOW (or series of WOWs) will be hugely expensive to you in the long run. I talked in the last chapter about how influential review websites can be, and in my experience there are broadly two types of people that share reviews on sites like Trip Advisor. The first are the type of people who enjoy blogging, likely to be active on Twitter and will enjoy posting one or more reviews, regardless of whether their stay was Nice, Disappointing Very Bad or WOW. The second are those guests who might blog occasionally but will typically only take time out to review when a stay has either WOWed them or was Very Bad, or so bad that they simply have to share with the world how terrible it was.

The obvious part that no business can ignore is that bad reviews will cost your business – in our case, bookings. These sites that share impartial thoughts and reviews will affect and influence booking decisions every single day. Bad reviews may be costing you money right now. These bad reviews get exponentially more powerful when there's a succession of them, all saying how rude the staff were, how bad the food was or how unhelpful the staff were in helping me with my problem with parking, getting to the airport on time, etc. You name it, if people are saying these bad things about your hotel, and the more there are saying the same thing, we move out of 'pinch of salt' territory to actively affecting booking decisions.

The current statistics from the most recent research at Cornell University states that 51% of guests check reviews before booking and 73% of those that check are directly impacted by those reviews. Let's run some numbers on this to see how impactful bad reviews are.

Let's assume that 500 guests are seriously considering booking with you. 49% do so without looking at any sort of review. That's 245 straightforward bookings.

51% check that review page – that's 255. Of those 255, 26%, despite checking, go on to book anyway. That's approximately 66 more bookings. That leaves 189 that will be directly impacted.

Let's assume that the average spend in the property is £150 per stay. That's £28,350. If you are not bothered to manage your reputation effectively on Trip Advisor you could be missing out on nearly £30k per month! Per year that is £340,200. Incidentally, The Wow Guest Management Course includes a day's training around reputation management and is considerably less than this!

You don't need to know the hard stats to be able to get a feel for how much money these bad reviews are costing. If in a given month you average 50 bookings via one of the major booking engines like booking.com, several hundred, if not thousand, users view your hotel's dedicated page on this site. Let's assume for round numbers that 1,000 users view these pages in a given month so you have a conversion rate of 5%. 950 users do not book, for a number of reasons that will be out of your control. Many are within your control. Let's assume just 10 – that's 1% – of users don't book as a direct result of seeing a succession of bad reviews all relating to the same thing. If the average revenue of a booking (including room, drinks, food, extras they spend with you) is £250; that's £2,500 a month in lost sales per month; £30,000 per year. And the reality is that 1% is probably far too low; it might be 2% (£60,000), 5% (£150,000) or even 10% (£300,000) that are influenced not to book as a direct result of these bad reviews. I accept these numbers are estimates based on assumptions, but the reality is that this is happening every day and the solution lies in your ability to put the customer experience right with a WOW Moment, or series of WOW Moments, to overcome this hugely expensive problem.

You only have to look at (and you should be looking at) what the biggest companies in the world do, and the lengths they go to get the customer experience right every single time, despite the challenges that need to be overcome along the way. I was at a talk with an entrepreneur in 2011 who used to be very senior at Amazon. He shared an experience that serves as a wonderful example of just how a WOW Moment can turn a bad or very bad experience into a lifelong customer. He explained that a customer had purchased a washing machine from Amazon and that it had arrived with some slight technical faults and, in short, didn't work as it should have done. When Amazon received the complaint, they picked up the washing machine the very next day and replaced it with another one, all at cost to them. Now a huge conglomerate like Amazon has the infrastructure and the capital to react in this way, but the same should be true in your hotel. There will be instances where you'll lose money from a guest staying with you to overcome a bad experience, but if it's implemented in the right way you'll not only turn that experience around, you'll also retain that customer for years to come. Because don't ever forget about the life of a customer. Your goal with every guest must be to get them to return or to refer.

A WOW brought back from a bad experience is most likely to make it to the dinner party. A WOW is nothing more than a demonstration that your guest's stay means a lot to you. If you can successfully demonstrate this, you'll soon find that whatever went wrong in the first place is soon forgotten (depending on what it is of course!). And it's worth emphasising again that this shouldn't, or shouldn't have to cost you much: the upgraded room is quite simply the easiest high perceived/low cost product you have – use it, as it's almost certain to make it to the next dinner party.

CHAPTER EIGHT

THE MORE YOU KNOW ABOUT YOUR GUESTS, THE MORE OPPORTUNITIES YOU HAVE TO WOW

Imagine for a moment that you own a local butcher's in a small community; you've just opened and are working hard to integrate yourself into the community. Customers drift in and out of your shop all day long: some purchase, some don't. Whether each person buys or not, they are a lead who is more likely to buy than someone who has never even heard of your shop. Now imagine that you knew the name, address and telephone number of each customer who walked in the door – not only that, but roughly when they would be walking through the door and precisely why they were there in the first place. Imagine you knew Mrs Jones was arriving at some point in the afternoon on Tuesday, you knew what she looked like, you knew that she was looking for four fillet steaks for her husband's 40th birthday. Think about the possibilities to WOW…

Well you might start by first preparing the steaks and dropping Mrs Jones a text message to let her know they were cut, prepared and ready for her; that you've chosen the very best meat and that they'll be perfect for her husband's birthday. When she arrived in the shop you'd greet her as welcomingly as possible and talk to her about where that particular cut has come from and why the quality is so good. You might also offer her a complimentary cook book, either one you had written yourself or from a reputable chef, about cooking with meat, or steak to be specific. You might offer Mrs Jones a discount coupon on her next purchase. You could advise a great red wine that goes with fillet steak that either you're selling yourself or that you know is stocked by a fantastic wine merchant down the road. Mrs Jones would leave feeling thoroughly looked after. But then a few days later you might drop her a text again or make a phone call to her and ask if her husband had had a good birthday and whether he enjoyed his steak.

Now I've never seen this level of service from a butcher, but if I did I would be spending an awful lot of money with them, wouldn't you? The bigger point, though, is that butchers and most businesses don't have this sort of information. You do. Every hotel in the world has basic information about customers that most bricks and mortar businesses would (or should) be biting your arm off to have, because the fundamental principle of every business is that the more you know about your customers, the more opportunities you have to WOW. Now there's plenty more info that you could be asking for, but let's first concentrate on the bread and butter, the basic details that you already have about your customers. Just to be clear, no extra work is required from you, no website changes, no extra systems, just using what you already have.

1. **Address** – Using the address was discussed under *WOW Moment 3 – Thank You Letter With Chocolates.* Send a letter before and after their stay.

2. **Mobile** – By now you will have cottoned on to just how important having their mobile number is. Sending a text message is *the most* immediate, unlikely to be ignored medium there is: start using it.

3. **Full Name** – Try to avoid using initials. The type of establishment you operate will determine whether you personalise your correspondence as 'Hi Sue' or 'Dear Mrs Jones'.

4. **Email** – You'll want to make sure this is added to your database, provided they have opted in to receive emails from you. You should be using this to not only welcome and confirm their booking but to keep an ongoing dialogue with them; hit them with a price point offer every once in a while that they can't ignore.

These four basic pieces of information open up wondrous opportunities to connect with your guests and build a relationship with them. They allow you to WOW, upsell and gain feedback and, most crucially of all, give you the opportunity to encourage a repeat booking.

If you're really wanting to WOW your guests and make it into the conversation at the next dinner party; you'll want to know the why. Why their staying with you will determine what you should be offering your guests, what they want from their stay and what they are likely to buy whilst staying with you. If it's a business trip for one night, pushing the use of your day spa probably isn't the best use of your resources; if you have a family with two small children all in the same room, offering them a romantic package with rose petals and Champagne probably isn't the way to go either. Certainly, if you have a couple on an anniversary, celebrating a birthday or a honeymoon, this is the type of thing you'll need to know if you want to make sure their stay is exactly as they imagined.

It really doesn't have to be difficult to do this. If they are booking via your own website, adding a simple mandatory tick box which asks what type of stay they are looking for will do the trick. You may also want to add an 'any special requirements' box, which you might find they use to not only tell you that it's their anniversary, but it's their silver wedding anniversary and they'd like a bottle of Champagne waiting for them in the room on arrival. You could try sending them a text or dropping them a phone call to explain their booking has been confirmed and enquire the reason for their stay. Phone calls can be time consuming, but there's no better way to start that relationship-building process. And if you're thinking that it might be a little intrusive to call – it won't be. The reason for your call is to reassure your guest that the booking has been received; this reassurance will always be well received.

Depending on what WOW Moments you're making available to your guests, you might want to make the wording more personalised to each guest and their specific stay. For example, if you have implemented the text message offering a free drink at the bar WOW Moment, it might read:

> Dear Mrs Jones, we hope you're enjoying your birthday stay. Please feel free to head down to the bar for a free birthday drink on us. Simply show this text message to Roberto who will gladly pour a drink of your choosing.

By the time Mrs Jones receives this text, she's probably forgotten that she even told your hotel that her visit was a birthday treat, thus the WOW is at its peak. To repeat, the fundamental point of doing these things is to demonstrate that you are prepared to do everything possible to make their stay as memorable as possible. Executed well, your guests will appreciate that you've made their special occasion extra special.

Research your guests. Go further and find out everything you can about them. This digital age presents a perfect opportunity to find out snippets of information about your guests that can be used to WOW them. Now bear with me because it might sound crazy (and frankly it should, because there's a whole world of mediocre hotels out there that would never dream of doing anything quite so daring), but the reality is that it won't take long (believe me it won't) and it doesn't have to be with every guest that stays with you. Here's what to do: take five minutes to Google your guest. If it's John Smith, it's probably not going to be too effective; if they've got an unusual name – go for it, see what comes up. For business guests, punch in their name on LinkedIn, find them and find what they do, who they work for, etc. Facebook might be worth a quick search as well, but I suspect that more opportunities will present themselves on Twitter. The type of things you should be looking out for are hobbies, interests, profession, blogs etc. It may sound a little intrusive, but remember this is all stuff in the public domain – you're not attempting to hack into their bank account! Spend five minutes, no more, and see what you can find. Better yet, take a pool of 10-20 guests with unusual names and use an outsourcing website like PeoplePerHour.com or fiverr.com to find a web researcher. I expect you can have 10 to 20 guests researched in an hour for less than £5. I use these sites all the time and once you've found a good freelancer it's an incredible asset to have.

Just to be clear, this information is not to be used to brief your receptionist to reel off everything you know about them as soon as they walk through the door! That might just scare them off. You're looking for snippets of information that can be used as a WOW Moment.

For example, if you were to search for me on Twitter my name is @adamhamadache – I have a relatively unusual name and you'll quickly identify me. Within 30 seconds, you can read my profile and learn that I'm the founder of The Wow Guest Group and that I support Liverpool Football Club. That's just from my 120 character profile; not through trawling through the hundreds of tweets to get a feel for me. A further 20 seconds on the internet would give you a list of all of Liverpool's forthcoming games and whether they're televised or not. If it happens that Liverpool are on the TV during my forthcoming visit and your in-house bar typically shows football imagine how I would feel if I received a text from the GM on my arrival letting me know that the Liverpool game would be playing in the bar at 5.30pm and if I'd like to head down and watch it there will be a free beer waiting for me. WOW. This would be really clever because if I've been offered a free drink to watch the game, I'm very unlikely to sit there for two hours and drink just one. I'll likely have two or three, order some nuts, maybe a sandwich. My total bill might be £20, the hard cost would likely be less than £1 to get me there *and* I feel thoroughly looked after by the hotel.

Here's another example. You have a young couple book a stay for a long weekend under the woman's name. You perform your basic searches and this time on LinkedIn you identify that she is the PA to a CEO of a large firm. You dig a little deeper and read that as part of her role she is required to book meeting rooms/conference facilities and that their head office isn't far away. What an opportunity. So you send her a letter and explain that you're delighted that they have decided to stay with you and that you would love the opportunity to show her around the conference facilities in exchange for a free meal at the restaurant. This is not so much a WOW Moment, but a wonderful opportunity to engage with a guest with some pretty impressive buying power and build a relationship from there. Plus you're offering her the opportunity to eat for free. A great opportunity if you are prepared for it.

Another important point I'd like to make: Twitter is your most powerful asset here. You'll no doubt have a profile on each of the major social media sites (if not, *why not?*). If I book a stay with you and you add me on Facebook or ask me to like the page, it's a little much, bearing in mind I've not visited yet. However if you follow me on Twitter and drop me a tweet along the lines of looking forward to having you stay with us, you've demonstrated that you have a genuine interest in my stay and you're committed to ensuring I have a great experience. Again, something that takes no time at all and can be implemented at any level.

My final point about information: databases. Your database is your most important asset in the business. It needs to be used and it needs to be used well. Remember that your business should be about the big four elements and of particular relevance to this point is the third:

1. Enhance the customer experience
2. Increase the average spend
3. Encourage repeat and referral bookings direct
4. Increase the amount of positive reviews

Your database is the best place to start to achieve this vital third point. Make sure there is a system in place that can capture all the details discussed in this chapter. That's:

- the basics – name, address, mobile, email, twitter
- the reason for stay – anniversary, birthday, business
- and the little bits of info about them – sports/teams they're into, their profession etc.

Get this all into the database and use it in the future.

If you aren't already using a customer relationship management system (CRM) then there are some suggestions available on www.wowguest.com/resources

You'll be able to use a CRM to set reminders of when important events are happening in your customers' lives. For example, if you know their birthday or anniversary, drop them an email or letter a month before, with some added value offer and explain that you'd be delighted if they were to stay with you to celebrate; as an extra incentive we'll even throw in our 'birth-day/anniversary package free of charge'.

If you are not currently utilising a CRM or database, here's something for you to think about. Imagine that you have £5,000 to spend on promoting Valentine's Day. You decide to run a targeted national press ad to drive new business into the hotel for that period. Now imagine that you have an extensive database full of 10,000 customers who have stayed with you in the last two years and you decide to use that £5k to target this group both via email and mail. You write a carefully worded piece of direct response marketing, with all the necessary measurable elements in place, create an offer and have it printed on quality stock to be sent out. Nine times out of 10, the previous guests will outper-form the ad because it's targeted, it's personalised and it's much easier to sell to those who have bought from you before, provided their experience was a positive one. These people are your lowest hanging fruit, ready to be picked, if you manage them properly.

- **Twitter** – profile page description; follow them from the hotel's account
- **LinkedIn** – what they do for a living, who they work for
- **Facebook** – does their profile picture suggest some sort of hobby or interest?
- **Google** – what comes up when you search for them? Do they have a blog, what do they blog about?

The types of things you should be looking out for are:

- Profession
- What magazines they like to read
- General interests – Buy the latest magazine in their interest and leave it on their bed with a note
- Cultural interests – theatre, architecture, museums, art galleries, fine dining: information on all the local versions of these
- Sports they like – are they showing when they are due to stay? If not in the bar, drop them a

text with the channel number on which they can get the live game on their TV in their room

- Sports teams they support
- Leisure sports they participate in – golf, fishing, swimming, cycling, tennis, squash, walking…
- Health and beauty interests or treatments
- Entrepreneurialism
- Stocks and Shares/Trading

Whilst the general formula is described above, this takes some consideration and will need to be thought about in each context. Plus, it can be time consuming and not applicable to each guest. Even if you can only manage two or three guests in this way every month, those 24-36 people per year will tell dozens more about how you went out of your way to enhance their experience.

CHAPTER NINE

Your Existing or Previous Guests Are The Best Source of New and Repeat Bookings

Until this point, the focus has almost solely been on the two of the three most important things this book covers – WOWing customers and increasing the average spend within the hotel. Now it's time for arguably the most commercially valuable element – repeat, direct bookings. These are the big wins because the cost of a repeat booking will typically be lower than that of a new booking and the margin will be higher, particularly if they book directly through your website so no meaty commission to pay to the OTAs.

So how to do it? Well there's a long list of ways, some of which we'll cover in this chapter, but I want to focus on the current customers who are about to leave your hotel. Reward quick action. This is what smart businesses do. If your customers book by X, stays within Y, they'll save Z. Typically X might be two weeks, Y might be 12 months and Z might be 50%. To get this great deal, though, guests will be required to pay up front; this will boost your cash flow and secure another booking. This method only really works with leisure guests, and bear in mind who your customers are. If we're talking about a cash-rich, affluent retired couple who short break 10 times a year, your response rate will be much higher than a not so affluent young family.

So how to do this? My advice is always try to differentiate the WOW Moment from the sales messages. If Mr and Mrs Jones had a lovely stay at Made Up Hotel, have been sufficiently WOWed and arrive home to find a letter from the GM thanking them for their visit, without a sales message, that's a really strong position to be in to then drop them an email a few days later with an enticement of a repeat booking for a great rate. Now this repeat booking may mean you'll see them in six, nine or even 12 months' time, but right *now* is the time to get them to commit because the WOW experience is fresh in their mind. So many hotels I see, week after week, simply watch their customers leave – many of them more than satisfied by their experience – and the only process they have in place is to add them to the generic newsletter that goes out once a month. It's not personalised, and it might go out 28 days after the guest has visited. Madness. By the way, this is all going on whilst the marketing team is coming up with new ideas to spend money on getting new customers. It's completely nuts – there is your target customer, waiting for that little nudge that makes them think they can't turn down a deal like that.

Here's another way of thinking about this. Right now, across the country and indeed across the world, there are former guests of your hotels saying things like, 'Oh we had such a wonderful time there, I'm just not sure why we haven't been back.' This is happening if not every day, then every week and certainly every month. But here's the crucial point – it's not your customers' job to remember how good a time they had and make decisive action to book and visit again. It's *your* job to remind them and incentivise them to visit again, over and over again, in an entertaining way that makes you stand out from the hundreds if not thousands of marketing messages they receive every day from other companies trying to flog them stuff.

Here's another myth that I must insist on dispelling about these occurrences: it has almost nothing to do with the recession. It has everything to do with the quality of your marketing. I won't labour this point, but it's important that this mindset is acknowledged because unsuccessful hoteliers will blame their poor sales on the recession when almost all the time it comes down to their ability to be able to market their services to the right people in the right way.

Another thing to consider when attempting to drive repeat bookings from your existing customers is that not all customers are created equal and they most certainly should not be treated as such. I can't tell you how many times I've listened to friends, family members, colleagues, clients, complete strangers talk about an organisation of which they are a customer, but feel undervalued and taken for granted; that only the new customers get the best deals and the best levels of service. It's so typical with mobile phone companies, gyms and leisure clubs. These rants are occurring because their service is backwards; they're treating their disloyal customers better than their loyal customers, just to get the sale. Madness. What's needed here is a system that recognises the loyal customers and treats them in a way that is preferential (or perceived to be preferential) to the new customers.

When it comes to marketing to your database, it's really quite simple – segmentation is the key. As soon as a customer has visited for the first time, make sure they know they are now part of an exclusive club of former guests. The language you use to describe the club should be elitist, superior, even downright snobbish, because you want your former guests to acknowledge that they are one of your absolute favourite customers, and they now belong to this community. I'd recommend even going a step further and creating an elite of the elite club: those guests who have stayed with you a few times now. A guest who has stayed with you more than twice, provided the experience was consistently enjoyable, is the type of guest that you'll want to bend over backwards for. The type of loyalty that these customers exhibit cannot be bought or swayed by a cheaper deal elsewhere; they love your hotel and wouldn't dream of going or staying anywhere else. I think we'd all like customers like that, wouldn't we? Think about them as silver, gold and platinum customers.

The type of content and frequency of contact should be different for each tier of customer. With the gold and silver customers you'll want to use statements like, 'as a valued customer' or 'as a member of our exclusive platinum membership'. Really hammer home that these customers are special. Your platinum member might even receive 25% discount in the bar, for example. Make them feel so valued that the idea of going anywhere else is completely inconceivable.

The bigger wins, however, will come from referrals. Word of mouth, as many agree, is the most powerful form of marketing. It's always easier to sell someone else than it is to sell yourself. So when a guest, having been suitably WOWed regales their friends at the dinner party, or down the pub or over coffee or wherever, with the tale of their remarkable experience at your hotel, you have a very real chance their of word of mouth marketing working for you – and it costs you nothing. But, as we all know, it's incredibly difficult to track, measure and control. Imagine for a second, however, that you *could* control your word of mouth marketing and successfully accrue approximately one to three new bookings for every satisfied guest. This would be an absolute breakthrough in word of mouth marketing!

WOW Moment 12 – Special Occasion Cards

Switched on hoteliers have their database segmented so they know how frequently each of their customers has visited and gives special attention to those customers who stay several times a year. Those customers are on the Christmas card list – a personal card from the GM wishing them a Happy Christmas. This won't harm your relations with these customers in the slightest.

Really switched on hoteliers, though, know who these customers are, but don't send a Christmas card. Think about it. The point of a gesture like this is to stand out and have the customer feel a little bit shocked that you've bothered to make an effort to contact them in such a personal way. But what happens in December? Your customers receive dozens of Christmas cards, each more beautiful and personal than the next. All of a sudden your (rather expensive) gesture has got lost amidst the barrage of friends, family and other businesses all competing for a moment of fond appreciation from your customer.

So, here's a tip – send a Christmas card in November. Have it read something like this:

Dear Mrs Jones,

You no doubt receive dozens of Christmas cards each year and we wanted to demonstrate that genuine thought went into this one, so we've made sure ours is the first one you receive this year.

A very merry Christmas to you and the family.

From the team and me at Made Up Hotel

Adam Hamadache
General Manager
Made Up Hotel

Cut through achieved. Money well spent.

Alternatively, send an Easter Card – you can almost guarantee that your guests won't receive one – make light of it and write something like:

Dear Mrs Jones

Happy Easter! We know it's a bit odd to send an Easter card but we wanted to wish you an enjoyable break nonetheless!

From the team and me at Made Up Hotel

Adam Hamadache
General Manager
Made Up Hotel

The Easter one is my favourite here; the way it's written basically explains that what we're doing by sending you this card is ridiculous but it was simply an opportunity to wish you well – that's a fantastic WOW.

Lastly, if you've got details of the guest's birthday or anniversary, get a card out to them to wish them happy birthday. Here's a nice way of thinking about it: your guest is probably a regular customer of several restaurants, several websites, a couple of airlines, a handful of bars, a butcher, a baker, a drycleaners, the list goes on and on. How many of these companies know your customer's birthday? And how many will bother to send a card? Set the bar for every other business your customer buys from and be the most stand out business of them all.

FREE DOWNLOAD

To download all the templates used in this book, and for a selection of my preferred suppliers, please visit

www.wowguest.com/resources

CHAPTER TEN

WITHOUT THE BASICS YOUR WOWS ARE WASTED

The simple fact of any hotel business is that if customer service is not of a suitable minimum standard, any WOW Moments that you attempt will be wasted. Every member of staff within the hotel must put the customer first. Nothing new, right? Well in every hotel there will be a set of systems and procedures that for 99% of the time will be the absolute right one, but 1% of the time it will completely defy common sense. The result is that if that procedure is adhered to the customer experience suffers. Let me give you an example: a friend of mine stayed in a hotel in Las Vegas some months ago; it is notably one of the newest and most luxurious hotels on the strip and certainly isn't cheap to stay in. My friend and his family were enjoying a typically hot Las Vegas day by the pool and asked the waitress if he could be brought some crisps, or 'chips 'n' dip' as the Americans say. The waitress kindly apologised and said that the chef had not brought any up from the kitchen to the pool area and as she was unable to leave the pool area, she was unable to help. Let's think about this for a second. You're relaxing by a pool in one of newest, most luxurious hotels in the world and the waitress has said she's unable to bring you a pack of crisps – doesn't make for great reading does it. It went on. She then explained that my friend could go to the other side of the resort and buy crisps himself if he wanted to. In the end I think he did, begrudgingly. Two people are at fault here:

1. The waitress hasn't had the initiative to dis-obey the system of not leaving the pool area for five minutes to meet the (very basic) needs of a customer.

2. The management team has not briefed their staff to do what is required to ensure their cus-tomers are seen to as they should be.

Incidentally, this story came to light when I asked what the hotel was like. He talked about some other stuff, but this stuck. The next time I visit Vegas and I come to choose a hotel, guess what will come to mind? This story, without a doubt.

This brings me onto my next point: if you are unable to meet your customers' most basic needs, the experience simply won't be a WOW (unless of course you have the bad experience system in place) You may have read, or heard of the book by Tim Ferris, *The 4 Hour Work Week*. Excellent read, I highly recommend. The gist is that Tim's goal is to not work any longer than is absolutely necessary. He starts a sports nutrition brand and automates the systems so that it works on its own, with companies briefed and ready to stock and supply the product to the customers. The point I want to highlight from Ferris' book is that once he knows he can trust his outsourced companies, he tells them that if there's any problem with an order or something goes wrong, he authorises them to spend $100 in favour of the customer. What a clever concept this is: the customer experience is more important than the profit made from a sale – something that many businesses would do well to remember.

On this point of focusing on the customer and not the sale, I'd like to share one of my own experiences at a very grand, luxurious country manor hotel. On arrival I checked in and was asked if I would like a newspaper in the morning. I said yes, I'd like *The Times* please. My choice was returned with an apology and information that they only provided *The Independent*. Hmm. Ok, well, I'll have to have *The Independent* then, won't I? When I came to check out, I noticed on the bill that I'd been charged £1.20 for *The Independent* – which I never wanted in the first place. Now let's be clear about this: if you are going to offer a newspaper to guests, allow them to make the choice. If it's a case of you have to have this or nothing, it's better not to offer in the first place. Second point to make here is that the margins on newspapers is so minute that the hotel might have made a few pence out of me, but severely tarnished my experience in the process. I had a lovely time other than that, but it left me with a bitter taste and I now find myself not recommending and unlikely to return. If you're currently offering a newspaper, don't dictate what your guest must read and certainly don't charge them for it!

Another fundamentally obvious point, but one I simply couldn't omit, is that friendly staff are essential. Remember the coffee shop example I gave in Chapter One. The key point here is that people like to deal with happy people, not miserable people, and if your staff are miserable, it doesn't matter what WOW techniques you use, you won't WOW your customers. What will happen is that a few days after departing your hotel, your guests will sit around the dinner table with friends and family and say something along the lines of, 'The hotel was amazing, they really looked after us, but the receptionist was so miserable!' All that time, effort and money spent on having WOWed your guest has been wasted. Here comes the challenging part about all of this: unless someone is overtly rude to your guests, you won't find out about it. Particularly in the UK; us Brits don't like to cause a fuss! What will happen is your guests will put up with misery guts on reception, or behind the bar, or by the pool and go home feeling satisfied but a little underwhelmed by their stay. This is why it is imperative to underpin an enthusiastic nature in your staff. As the GM or hotelier, it is your responsibility to choose staff who are willing to be friendly to guests; and it is also your responsibility to maintain that enthusiasm and friendliness.

My last point concerns your fundamental procedures that don't necessarily have anything to do with customer service, but refer to the most basic principles of your hotel. I'm talking about booking confirmation and the room you've allocated actually being vacant (believe me it happens!). Fail to do these most basic of tasks and all the effort your WOW Moments require will be wasted. I'll finish with another bad experience shared by a friend. He arrived at a hotel having pre-booked a parking space in the car park, paying a small premium for this additional service. When he arrived, there were no parking spaces. A little annoyed, he spoke to receptionist who informed him that they couldn't actually guarantee a free parking space, despite that fact that he had paid for it. What a start. Needless to say, he won't be visiting again, and he won't be recommending that his friends stay there either.

WOW Moment 13 – Car Park Greeting

If your hotel is not centrally located and has a car park used by most guests, pay attention to this WOW Moment, because it represents an opportunity to WOW your guests before they've even walked through the door.

First point: when your customer is booking, ask them if they wish to use the car park during their stay; if so, what is the registration number plate of the car they will be arriving in. Some guests may be booking way in advance, or plan to rent a car and won't necessarily know this information. That's ok, just don't make it a mandatory field throughout the booking process.

Second point: collate and print out the names and the corresponding registration numbers of the guests who will be arriving each day. Make sure this is listed in alphabetical order in terms of registration number.

Third point: have that list with the concierge or at reception. This works best when you have a CCTV camera showing cars entering the car park. When the designated member of staff sees a car entering the car park, he/she quickly identifies the name of the guest who the car belongs to. They head into the car park and greet the guest with the following sentence:

'Good afternoon, Mr Hamadache, welcome to Made Up Hotel, can I help you with your bags?'

This is one of my favourite WOW Moments. What a WOW! Not even Claridges or the Dorchester does this; nor does Atlantis in Dubai. No guest will ever expect this and it is one of the most powerful demonstrations that:

a) You're a switched on hotel
b) You put the guest first
c) Your staff are exceptionally helpful and friendly

This doesn't have to happen with every guest. Not every guest will give you their car registration number for a start. Also, what happens when five cars arrive at once and you only have one or two staff free to perform this WOW Moment? In this case, do nothing, you don't want to be showing favouritism to one guest. WOW Moments are about valuing your customer, not about making one customer feel less valued than another. If your staff can perform this task 10 to 12 times per day (it takes two minutes) then the best part of 4,000 guests per year will tell that story over and over again. That's powerful.

The registration number example above is a great WOW, but it only works when all the elements are in place. A less powerful, but easily implemented way to WOW on arrival, is have your staff greet the guest in the car park and take their bags. If you have a luggage trolley in the hotel, even better. The bags get wheeled into the hotel and guests walk leisurely into reception; excited about the welcome they've just received.

WOW Moment 14 – Umbrellas

Part One

Umbrellas. No gesture will be more welcome to a guest, particularly a female guest, who has forgotten an umbrella when it's tipping it down.

Adding to the WOW of greeting in the car park, you'll want your guests to stay dry. Have your greeter armed with a couple of large golf-size umbrellas to hand to the guests when they step out of the car into the rain. What a wonderful illustration that you're a thoughtful hotel that genuinely cares about your guests.

Part Two

If your guests are venturing out for the day, in the rain, and they don't have an umbrella, why not give one to a guest to keep? Or if they're leaving the hotel having completed their stay, hand them one on their way out. Think about it: it will be branded with your hotel's name and number (use a tracking number here); you're giving your guest the opportunity to advertise your hotel for the cost of £3-4 when you buy in bulk. Better yet, up your base rate stays by £3 during rainy months of the year to cover the cost. Not only is this exceptionally clever marketing, it's also a fantastic WOW Moment that serves as a welcome parting gift.

WOW Moment 15 – Late Arriving Call

Most days you are likely to have guests who arrive later than expected, or perhaps after the kitchen closes. The clever thing to do here is have your reception team pick up the phone and ask the guest how they're getting on, do they need directions etc. It also presents a unique opportunity to upsell. Have your receptionist mention that the kitchen is closing in 15 minutes so if they are likely to be hungry when they arrive, they could order something now and have it sent up to their room on arrival. Not only is this a personal, unexpected and thoughtful gesture, it will consistently increase your F&B revenue. All done at a time when your staff are likely to be doing very little!

WOW Moment 16 – Drink On Arrival

I have a vivid memory of a family holiday I had when I was about 11 and we went to the very beautiful island of Mauritius. We were there for two weeks, but looking back I have maybe three or four memories that I've taken from that time. One of them is being welcomed into the hotel with a very fruity, delicious, non-alcoholic cocktail whilst the receptionists were seeing to our booking. That's a great WOW Moment. It was the perfect gesture to be greeted with on arrival to that very tropical hotel. Now, this WOW Moment won't be suitable for every hotel, but if your core clientele are families and leisure breakers, and you have ample seating area in your lobby to be able to offer something delicious that the customer can taste – it might be a fruit juice, it might be a freshly baked snack of some kind, the core principle is to demonstrate what your hotel is about (remarkable service) and provide a memory that will stand out when they look back on that visit months and years from now. Give it a go.

WOW Moment 17 – A Brief History…

I've mentioned several times the importance of that first touch point, when your guest steps into the hotel for the first time and goes through the check in process. What I often find is that, as good as the service is, there's always that minute or two of waiting whilst the receptionist prepares the key, checks the order, etc. This has happened in almost every hotel I have ever visited, and it represents a wonderful opportunity to WOW and begin the relationship building process. When I've stayed in a beautiful, country manor hotel, I've often thought it would be quite nice to know a brief history of the building, so I end up asking someone at the restaurant, the bar, the spa etc, and usually they don't know a thing! If your hotel has a story behind it, it's not the kind of thing you should be keeping to yourself; have someone on reception filling that two minutes of patient waiting with a brief history. I've stayed at hotels that were once slept in by King Henry VIII, but I've only found out afterwards from a friend. Provide your guests with an arsenal of memories that they can share with their friends and, if the building's story is compelling enough, it'll make it to the dinner party.

WOW Moment 18 – Origami Toilet Roll And Towel Swans

Your guests have arrived, the check in was good, they've walked into their room, they dump their bags, then what happens? They check out the bathroom. Everyone I know does it. What they typically find is the toilet roll folded over like an arrow. A nice touch, if the arrow is straight that is (which it's often not). This represents an opportunity to WOW. Imagine an intricate origami folding of the toilet roll waiting for them, or a towel spread across the bed, expertly engineered into two swans. Off the top of my head, I can think of at least one hundred people who would take a picture of that, pop it on Facebook, to show what they have found whilst checking in so all their friends know where they are staying. It all sounds complicated, but this is one of the cheapest WOW Moments – simply visit www.wowguest.com/resources for videos and links of how to do this. Spend 30 minutes teaching your maids how to do it, track their progress and you're ready to start WOWing your guests when they enter their room.

WOW Moment 19 – Kids In Room: Something To Entertain Them

If you take the time to understand your guests, you'll know, broadly, who they are and what they're visiting for. Imagine that you know that a family of four is visiting and the two children are aged between four and seven. You know this because that information is part of the booking process. In every room you may have a mini bar – full of snacks and alcohol, not the things that Mum and Dad want to be paying for their children to consume, let alone a premium for the convenience. Take out all the alcohol and replace with fruit juice, chocolate and healthy snacks, as well as a selection of family films, games, books, etc. You won't necessarily have to let your guests know that you'll make this service available to them but when the parents find out, won't they be delighted? Even if you don't have minibar facilities, by demonstrating an understanding of your customer and offering a welcome service that keeps the kids entertained for a few minutes, your guests will be pleasantly surprised and WOWed.

WOW Moment 20 – Name, Not Room At Breakfast

This is a small one, but when I visit hotels and head down to breakfast and I'm asked what my room number is, it doesn't convey that I'm an important customer, does it? If I was asked for my name, I'd feel a little more valued than 'just another number'. That also gives the host the opportunity to say things like, 'Right this way, Mr Hamadache', which gives a much more personal touch to the experience.

This can be taken even further with what some hotels refer to as a 'look book' – it's simply a collection of images of important guests, perhaps those of your guests staying in the top suites, for example. Some of the top hotels will have daily team meetings to refresh and recap those VIP guests who reside in the look book, just so when they happen to bump into a maid in the hallway, or pop down to the bar for a G&T, they're greeted by name. I've seen this executed beautifully in some of the top five stars properties in London and the result is simply WOW, despite expectations being sky high. If you own or run a hotel that's not a five star, just imagine the impact it will have on those high-paying guests of yours…

WOW Moment 21 – 'Vegas' Postcard

If your guests are typically visiting for a leisure break or a holiday, this one is certainly for you. It stems from a hotel on the strip in Las Vegas I stayed at several years ago. This hotelier was quite smart because, as a free service to his guests, he offered to provide and send as many postcards as the guest required, paying for all the postage. What this meant was that the guests were WOWed by an unexpected WOW Moment that could cost them $10 or even $20 by the time they'd done friends and family members. The manager would specially prepare a postcard, illustrating an exclusive offer available to friends and family members of his previous guests, with a website link to find more detail and to book. It proved to be an incredibly powerful marketing tool.

There's nothing stopping you from doing this in your hotel, particularly if you are in a touristy area like the Lake District, the Cotswolds or Cornwall. Think about the WOW Moment made to your existing guest and the potential for new business that comes at a cheaper cost than the typical customer acquisition cost. Simply genius.

Final Thought

WOWing guests will have a profound impact on your hotel business – be it via indirect bookings or direct increase in F&B revenue. But there's more you can be doing to ensure that your hard-earned WOW Moments are truly reaching their absolute maximum potential. It's what I call leverage.

Without leverage, you leave your WOW Moments to chance, hoping that the increase in conversation about your hotel, and those warm fuzzy feelings you evoke in your guests, will ramp up your bottom line. Leverage falls into four disciplines – four areas that sadly, in my experience, hotels fall short on time and time again, as they fall straight into the pitfalls, become frustrated and make statements like 'social media doesn't work for us' and 'Trip Advisor is a nightmare'. These statements are a bit like putting a car in neutral and claiming that it doesn't work. Like anything, you must learn how to use it effectively to see the best results.

The four areas of concern are:

1. Guest Loyalty
2. Reputation Management
3. Social Media
4. Public Relations

When a deep understanding of these four disciplines has been developed, and an understanding of how to use them effectively, the power and impact on your WOW Moments will multiply by the nth degree.

1. Guest Loyalty

It's fair to say that retaining guests and keeping them loyal has never been harder. The choice and the competition for hotel rooms has never been fiercer; with the OTAs demanding low prices, it seems everyone is competing on price – great for the customer but not so great for business, particularly the independent hotels. Thankfully, there are techniques that, when intertwined with WOW Moments, can encourage more of those elusive repeat bookings. It stems from encouraging your guests to feel a part of a 'community'. Imagine that every person falls into one of three categories: never stayed with you, first timers and stayed with you more than once. Making a real fuss about the fact that it's a guest's first, second, third time of staying with you, combined with carefully executed incentives will soon encourage your guest to only ever look at one place for their next leisure or business trip.

2. Reputation Management

If the statement above about Trip Advisor resonated with you, I'm afraid you're going to have to embrace it or it's going to become a bigger and more impactful stress and burden in your life. The only way is up for Trip Advisor and, put simply, seeing it as an asset is an absolute necessity. Managing your reputation online isn't difficult, but there is a great deal to learn and with their algorithm changing regularly, as well as new features being added all the time, learning how to manage your reputation online from the experts should be a priority for any hotelier. Equally as important is the way you utilise Trip Advisor across your WOW Moments. A well-administered WOW Moment shared on Trip

Advisor will make for great reading for any prospective guest looking to book with you. Sadly, though, those odd couple of booking-driving anecdotes will play little part if your ranking is not doing your hotel justice.

3. Social Media

Social media probably has the most immediate power to leverage your WOW Moments. Displaying a towel swan elegantly across the bed will be shared on Facebook, Twitter, Instagram and many other websites. Not being active on social media is like being invited to a really fun party, walking over to the corner, facing the wall and putting your fingers in your ears whilst petulantly singing 'I can't hear yooooooooou'. Start delivering WOW Moments and your guests will start to share images, videos, anecdotes, and you'll want to be there to witness and leverage the public display of WOW that's helping you to drive more sales. Having a strategy is important to achieve specific objectives, though. Not having one can render the effort a little pointless.

4. Public Relations

Lastly, public relations and becoming known for something fits well with Chapter Two about the expectations of your guests. If the communication you broadcast oversells your hotel, your guest is likely to be underwhelmed and those WOW Moments run the risk of being wasted. Similarly, underselling yourself won't do you any favours either! Striking the balance can be tough, but getting it right can make a huge impact on your guest experience and your profitability.

Sadly, though, perhaps the biggest challenge of all is that the top experts and consultants ain't cheap! Bringing in the industry's brightest can leave a sizable dent in your budget. When I started in the industry, I set myself a challenge of finding a way of helping hoteliers access the very top expertise at a fraction of the cost of bringing them in individually.

The WOW Guest Programme does just that. It's a management-training course for independent hoteliers to help deliver WOW Moments and get trained by some of the leading experts from across the world in the four key areas to achieve that all important leverage.

For more information please visit

www.wowguest.com

THANK YOU

As a THANK YOU for reading *Give Your Guest A WOW!* I'd like to grant you access to exclusive interviews and training sessions with these leading experts, all for FREE.

To gain access to this invaluable material, just visit **www.wowguest.com/membersarea**

You'll need the following username and password to log in:

Username: **MyThankYou**

Password: **EnjoyTheContent**

I do hope you find it useful, and remember that a WOW Moment is nothing more than a gesture that's personal, unexpected and shows you appreciate your guests' custom. Good luck to you and your hotel.

THE AUTHOR

Adam is best known for creating The Wow Guest Programme – a hotel management training course that, over a 21-week period, draws on the expertise of leading figures across five key areas every hotel needs in order to drive more direct bookings.

As founder of The Wow Guest Group, his vision is to empower hotels to deliver experiences that WOW to create word of mouth marketing that drives more repeat and referral bookings, coming through directly to the hotel.

Since 2008, Adam has been commissioned by national newspapers in the UK to create hotel offers that drive bookings. In this time he's held contracts with over 600 hotels across the UK including the likes of Marriott, Best Western and Hilton.

Adam speaks regularly at hotel industry events including The Hotel Summit, and The Hospitality Exchange, as well as running his own seminars and workshops. He is also a regular columnist in *Hotel Owner* Magazine and publishes his own monthly *Wow Guest* newsletter, packed with valuable hints and tips to help hoteliers drive more direct bookings.

To request a free copy of the most recent newsletter, simply visit www.wowguest.com/newsletter

To connect with Adam, tweet him at @adamhamadache or email adam@wowguest.com

4800940R00095

Printed in Great Britain
by Amazon.co.uk, Ltd.,
Marston Gate.